American Academy of Religion Academy Series

Edited by
Carl A. Raschke

Number 51

ELOQUENCE AND IGNORANCE IN AUGUSTINE'S
ON THE NATURE AND ORIGIN OF THE SOUL
by
Mary C. Preus

Mary C. Preus

ELOQUENCE AND IGNORANCE IN AUGUSTINE'S ON *THE NATURE AND ORIGIN OF THE SOUL*

Scholars Press
Atlanta, Georgia

ELOQUENCE AND IGNORANCE IN AUGUSTINE'S
ON THE NATURE AND ORIGIN OF THE SOUL

by
Mary C. Preus

© 1985
American Academy of Religion

Library of Congress Cataloging in Publication Data

Preus, Mary.
  Eloquence and ignorance in Augustine's On the nature and origin of the soul.

  (American Academy of Religion dissertation series ; no. 51)
  Thesis (Ph.D.)—University of Minnesota, 1983.
  Bibliography: p.
  1. Augustine, Saint, Bishop of Hippo. De natura et origine animae. 2. Soul—Early works to 1800.
  3. Knowledge, Theory of (Religion)—Early works to 1800.
  I. Tithe. II. Series.
  BR65.A6852P74 1985   233'.5   85-19613
  ISBN 0-89130-927-6 (alk. paper)

Printed in the United States of America
on acid-free paper

MAGISTRIS

O.W. QUALLEY

BILL K. ADDISON

CONTENTS

ABBREVIATIONS AND CITATIONS

I. The following abbreviations are used in this dissertation:

A. DNOA - *De Natura et Origine Animae* of St. Augustine
B. Other works of St. Augustine:
   Cat.Rud. - *De Catechizandis Rudibus*
   CD - *De Civitate Dei*
   Conf. - *Confessiones*
   DDC - *De Doctrina Christiana*
   Ep. - *Epistulae*
   De Gen. - *De Genesi ad Litteram*
   De Mag. - *De Magistro*
   Retr. - *Retractationes*
   Solil. - *Soliloquies*
   De Trin. - *De Trinitate*
C. Works by other ancient authors:
   De An. - Tertullian's *De Anima*
   De Princ. - Origen's *De Principiis*
D. Editions or translations:
   ACW - Ancient Christian Writers
   ANF - The Ante-Nicene Fathers
   BA - Bibliothèque augustinienne
   CCL - Corpus Christianorum Latinorum
   CSEL - Corpus Scriptorum Ecclesiasticorum Latinorum
   FOC - Fathers of the Church
   LLA - Library of Liberal Arts
   PL - Patrologia Series Latina
   PNF - The Nicene and Post-Nicene Fathers
E. Other abbreviations:
   JTS - *Journal of Theological Studies*
   LXX - Septuagint
   NT - New Testament
   OT - Old Testament
   REA - *Revue des études augustiniennes*
   RSV - Revised Standard Version

II. Citations

    A.   From DNOA: Book and smaller chapter are listed. Larger chapter divisions are omitted as superfluous, e.g., IV,39 instead of IV,24,39. All translations are mine. Wherever a number appears with no work named (e.g., IV,39), the citation is from DNOA.

    B.   From Augustine's other works: Those cited frequently are listed above in the abbreviations. Location of the Latin text and the English translation used will be found in the Bibliography. For other works mentioned in the text, see accompanying footnote for location of Latin text and translation.

CHRONOLOGICAL TABLE

The following dates in Augustine's life are referred to in the dissertation or are pertinent to its argument:

354 - Augustine's birth.

373 - Reading of Cicero's *Hortensius*.

374 - Conversion to Manichaeism.

383 - Disillusionment with Manichaeism.

384 - Appointment to professorship of rhetoric in Milan.
Brief interest in Academic scepticism.

386 - Reading of the *libri platonici*.
"*Tolle lege*" episode (about 2 months after *libri platonici*).

387 - Baptism as a Catholic.

391 - Ordination.

395 - Consecration as Bishop.

396 - *De Doctrina Christiana*, Books I-III.

397–401 - The *Confessions*.

401–414 - *De Genesi ad Litteram*.

405 (?) - *De Catechizandis Rudibus*.

410–417 (?) - *De Trinitate*.

413–426 - *City of God*.

415 - Letter 166 to Jerome on the creationist question.

418 - Letter 190 to Optatus on the origin of the soul.

419–420 - *De Natura et Origine Animae*.

419 or early 420 - Letter 202A to Optatus.

426–427 - *De Doctrina Christiana*, Book IV.

430 - Augustine's death.

INTRODUCTION

One must undertake a dissertation on such a writer as St. Augustine with humility and trepidation. His own works are so numerous and varied that one despairs almost of reading all that he wrote, let alone all that has been written about his life and work. And what can one say that is new about a figure who has been a favorite subject of scholars, theologians, philosophers, classicists, and historians for fifteen centuries? It is perhaps too much to hope to make a new discovery; yet the fact that St. Augustine continues to inspire a steady flow of books, articles, even television shows,/1/ assures the student that this is a man worth studying, that even his minor writings will reward the researcher with some understanding of that compelling personality.

Relatively little has been written about *De Natura et Origine Animae*/2/ for some obvious reasons: it was not conceived as a unity, it is repetitious, and it covers ground already gone over in other more elaborate works, especially *De Genesi ad Litteram*. Moreover, it is directed, point by point, against a lost work of a writer otherwise unknown to us. Only in Book IV does Augustine depart from this rigid plan of point-by-point refutation and address a broader topic.

The only English translation of this treatise is found in the Nicene and Post-Nicene Fathers Series and dates from 1874. The translation is a good one, but there are almost no notes. It was in making a new translation with accompanying commentary that I was struck by one persistent theme: Augustine's play on the subject of knowledge and ignorance. *De Natura et Origine Animae* is certainly not an epistemological treatise like, for example, *De Magistro*; yet it is full of classical and Biblical ideas about self-knowledge and the limits of knowledge. Augustine's combination of classical and Scriptural assumptions about knowledge and ignorance is one step in the long and fascinating progression from Socrates' ironic protestations of ignorance to the *"docta ignorantia"* of the Middle Ages./3/

The tracing of the knowledge-ignorance theme (a question of philosophy) and the wish to comment in detail upon the writing style of this treatise (a question of rhetoric) pointed me toward examining DNOA as an Augustinian case study in the long history of conflict between philosophy and rhetoric. Augustine, like many other early Christian thinkers (pagan as well), experienced a conversion *away from* rhetoric *to* philosophy./4/ To his mind, the change signified a turning away from vanity, emptiness, and the material toward wisdom, substance, and the spiritual; away from *verba* toward *res*. However, this early negative view of rhetoric mellowed as Augustine's career forced him away from the philosophic life of individualistic, or at least cloistered, contemplation and into an active public position of authority, where teaching and the business of persuasion—spoken and written—occupied nearly all his time. His enormous public responsibilities necessitated attention to rhetoric and to the power of *verba*.

The two elements just mentioned—the knowledge/ignorance theme and the use of and attitude toward rhetoric—are the foundations on which I will construct this study of *De Natura et Origine Animae*. They are not unrelated, as the next few paragraphs should make clear.

A late work (420), *De Natura et Origine Animae* shows great attention to rhetoric and is an example of Augustine's care in the use of words and the devices of argumentation. Through studying it, I wish to show that the rhetor's life, which Augustine had at first ostensibly abandoned as a pagan relic, incompatible with the Christian vocation, reappeared, as though baptized, in response to the challenges of heresy and ignorance. My contention is that the old Platonic conflict between rhetoric and philosophy becomes in Christian terms the tension between the active and the contemplative life, and that Augustine's career represents a kind of solution to that tension. Three traditions direct his thought about the relationship of words to true knowledge: the Platonist, Ciceronian, and Scriptural traditions.

The relation of rhetoric to philosophy—of words to knowledge—was no mere academic question for Augustine. This brilliant and learned orator was also a bishop, a *Seelsorger*. In his anxiety for the salvation of souls, Augustine turned scholarship and rhetoric toward a pragmatic purpose: the conversion of his hearers. He thus gave much thought to the arts of instruction and persuasion. With

De Catechizandis Rudibus (somewhere between 399 and 405) he outlined his teaching methods for one of his deacons. But even earlier, in 396, he had undertaken *De Doctrina Christiana*, a guide to Biblical interpretation, and he considered the subject so important that he enlarged the work by an additional book 31 years later.

Augustine's methods of argumentation in DNOA—his plea of ignorance, his defense of suspended judgment, his use of sarcasm, his love of showy language, his alternation of praise and blame— illustrate admirably his own advice from the foregoing two books of rhetorical instruction. Teaching, if it is to be effective, requires imagination, identification with the pupil, and variety./5/ The pupil's delight in hearing (what Aristotle subsumes under *"ethos"* and Cicero under *"delectare"*) will mirror the teacher's delight in the truth that he teaches./6/ So Augustine, former professor of rhetoric, writes to the budding orator Vincentius not for the academic exercise in speculative philosophy but for the practical aim of converting his adversary. He does not look for victory in the debate as a triumph of personal authority or superior knowledge but as a contribution toward "saving knowledge" for Victor. His *"noli credere . . ."* to Victor is a piece of pragmatic advice.

In DNOA Augustine uses all his rhetorical skill to direct Vincentius toward "saving knowledge" or "true philosophy." The rhetoric-knowledge connection is perhaps more obvious than one other which needs to be made, viz., how to account for the prominence of the knowledge/ignorance theme in a treatise on the origin of the soul. Again the reason for digressing on knowledge seems to be Augustine's concern for the safety of Vincentius's soul. Just as the rhetorician is especially susceptible to pride, so the man who claims to know the answers to insoluble problems has succumbed to pride. Augustine's contention is that the soul's origin is an insoluble problem because of the limitations of human knowledge. In claiming to solve the problem and in ridiculing Augustine's indecision, Victor has in a sense reenacted the sin of Adam, transgressing the limits of knowledge in the belief that the serpent's seductive words, "You shall be like God, knowing good and evil," (Gen. 3:4–5) are true. Adam's sin, and so the primal human sin and root of all subsequent sin, is pride. Victor, like Adam, reaches for the forbidden fruit— complete knowledge. Victor's fundamental error, which Augustine treats first and most extensively, is making the human soul "like God" in the sense of being a particle of God, what Augustine in *De*

Genesi ad Litteram (VIII,14,31) calls *perversa imitatio Dei*. Thus the knowledge which Victor claims to possess is deceptive and pernicious because its root is *superbia*.

The first chapter of the thesis will examine Augustine's attitude toward rhetoric vis-à-vis philosophy. The second introduces the arguments of DNOA and could serve as a reader's summary of the treatise. The third chapter looks at the striking use of Socratic phrasing and ironic questioning in Book II, "knowing what you do not know." Book IV of DNOA again picks up the theme of knowledge, but this time directed inward. One is transported back to the introspective thought-world of the *Confessions* even though this is a much later work. The fourth chapter examines this book's version of "Know thyself," relating Augustine's thoughts to classical and Biblical antecedents. These four chapters do not expound Augustine's whole theory of knowledge; rather, they show how this theory finds distinctive expression in DNOA. The last chapter, Chapter 5, returns to a more comprehensive look at the entire treatise as a rhetorical and polemical exercise. If one were to fit this chapter into the knowledge/ignorance scheme, its title ought perhaps to be "Know thine adversary," for Augustine plainly adopts the style of argument appropriate to each of his correspondents, a principle which he had commended in both *De Catechizandis Rudibus* and *De Doctrina Christiana*. Chapters 1 and 2 are general background for the intelligent reading of DNOA; 3 and 4 have a more particular point; and 5 is again an overview of the whole treatise.

Historical Background

Albert de Veer has pieced together the most thorough account of the historical setting of DNOA./7/ The central character, to whom Books III and IV are directed, is a certain Vincentius Victor, a resident of Mauretania Caesariensis. From our treatise (I,2) we learn that Victor had recently left the sect of the Donatist Church called Rogatist and come over to the Catholic Church. His connection with the Rogatists identifies him more closely with the region of Mauretania around Cartenna (Tenes). His admiration for the late Rogatist bishop there, Vincentius, had led him to adopt his name, an action Augustine found unsuitable for a Catholic (III,2). Although a young man and a layman, Victor showed a natural eloquence (I,3) and a commendable acquaintance with Scripture

(III,21)—qualities which Augustine was anxious to see used in the service of true religion.

Victor first came to Augustine's notice as the author of two books, now lost to us, challenging what he considered to be a lamentable lack of forthrightness from the "experts" in answering the question of the soul's origin (IV,2). The Bishop of Hippo was his particular target for two reasons:

1) because Augustine confessed ignorance of whether the human soul was bestowed through propagation or through an individual creative act of God and
2) because he asserted that the soul was not a corporeal entity (*corpus*) but a spirit.

The particular piece of writing which Victor found so offensive is identifiable, by clues of place and persons, as Letter 190, composed in 418 by Augustine to a Mauretanian bishop, Optatus,/8/ regarding the origin of the soul. Optatus had not written to Augustine but had sent an inquiry on the problem to a conference of bishops meeting in Caesarea, Mauretania. Since Augustine was in attendance, the request was referred to him by the monk Renatus, who urged him to reply, as did another priest named Muresis, a relative of Optatus. Augustine's letter cautions Optatus against any dogmatic assertion about how souls are created: Scriptural texts are ambiguous and all the possible views of the soul's origin involve their defenders in dangerous theological difficulties over the related questions of original sin, the nature of the soul, and the problem of evil. It is this caution which aroused the scorn of Victor and emboldened him to attack Augustine by name (I,1).

The lay brother Renatus, mentioned above as bringing Optatus's letter to Augustine's attention, fulfilled the same service in respect to Victor's treatise. Acting both from apparent interest in the subject and from friendship and personal regard (I,1; I,35), he forwarded a copy of Victor's work to Hippo. Augustine was on a journey at the time (I,1), but he considered the matter important enough to reply to Renatus as soon as he returned./9/ His letter mentions that he intends to write to Victor himself (I,34), thus indicating that the order in which we have the four books of *The Nature and Origin of the Soul* is the order of their composition.

The third recipient of Augustine's letters on the topic was a Spanish priest, Peter. In his house Victor had come upon the "little work" of Augustine's that had prompted his criticism (II,18). Peter encouraged his protégé to write down his views and was so enthralled with the results that at the public reading of the book he embraced the author and exclaimed how much he had learned (II,1; perhaps an eyewitness account from Renatus). What, exactly is it that he has learned?, Augustine inquires sarcastically, taking the priest to task for being so misled by his young friend's eloquence (II,1–5; II,21).

Peter's Spanish origin may account for some of Victor's theological tendencies. Augustine accuses Victor (III,9) of favoring the Priscillianist heresy: viz., that the soul achieved some meritorious status before its union with the body. This revival in Spain of Origen's belief in the soul's preexistence/10/ Augustine deplored in his treatise *Contra Priscillianistas* and in the single book addressed to Orosius, another Spaniard./11/

The Creationist-Traducianist Controversy

Victor found it ludicrous that a scholar of Augustine's reputation (*doctissimus . . . expers*) should have avowed ignorance on a question so basic as where our souls come from. In his attack, Victor taunted the Bishop with a verse from Psalm 48/49, comparing him with "senseless cattle." The gibe probably irritated Augustine all the more because he had repeatedly begged Jerome for his help on the question, without success./12/ Therefore, in DNOA he defended his right to withhold judgment on an issue which he felt it might be hubris to try to solve (IV,5) and which was, in any case, of secondary importance; it is far more urgent for us to know our soul's destiny than its origin (IV,14).

The reason that Augustine was so unwilling to express an opinion on the origin of the soul was that any theory carried with it certain unacceptable implications. In a letter to Jerome/13/ he once listed four possible opinions:

1) souls are propagated, like bodies, from the first man—the theory called traducianism
2) souls are created anew for each single person—the theory called creationism
3) souls are sent into bodies by God from some preexistent state
4) souls go into bodies of their own accord.

Reluctance to admit a preexistent soul kept Augustine from considering the last two alternatives seriously;/14/ his difficulty lay in choosing one of the first two, although he was impressed by Jerome's support for creationism. Naturally the advocates of either view based their claim on Scripture, but Augustine easily demonstrated that every Scriptural text offered as proof of one position could just as well be interpreted in favor of the other (I,17–20). A worse problem was that either position would apparently violate either "human reason or divine authority" (I,16).

Since divine authority seemed unlikely to settle the question directly, Augustine was forced to look for a choice acceptable in the light of those doctrines which Scripture teaches unequivocally. The most important of these bearing on the soul's origin was the doctrine of original sin. The Biblical witness of Romans 5:12–19 constituted proof of the universality and hereditary nature of human sin (IV,16). But equally compelling, to Augustine's mind, was the argument from the Church's long-established practice of infant baptism: why would the Church baptize infants "for the remission of sins" unless they were sinners even at birth, before they could have committed any personal sins? The Pelagians, who denied original sin, had been officially condemned by the Church only a year before our treatise, in 418. Augustine's battle with them, which was to last until the end of his life, had primed him for violent opposition to any theological formulation which seemed to make light of human bondage to sin. Hence the appeal for him of the traducianist argument, which conveniently explained the passing on of sin from Adam to his descendants.

The theory was not, however, free from difficulties, the most embarrassing of which was its apparently necessary link with the teaching of the soul's corporeality. It would be difficult to conceive of an incorporeal soul's being passed on through a corporeal medium, Augustine confesses to Optatus in Epistle 190,15. The Bishop rejects the crude materialism of Tertullian, who even called God *corpus*./15/ So although Augustine sees that traducianism provides the best *logical* accompaniment to the doctrine of original sin, nevertheless when it comes to making a defense, his heart is not in it. In fact, he admits straight out in *De Genesi ad Litteram* X,1, that his inquiry there concerning the soul's origin will "carefully seek how we may or may not refute those who believe that the soul comes from the soul of the first man."/16/ He pleads with Jerome

to give him unambiguous proof in support of the latter's creationist preference and seems almost embarrassed to name the alternative./17/

Creationism propounds the incorporeality of the soul, breathed
out by an incorporeal God. But again original sin rears its ugly head.
If souls come into being through God's direct action, how are we to
escape making God responsible for their sinful state (I,6–7 and 16)?
Victor tries to evade the difficulties of the theory but falls headlong
into contradiction. He asserts that the soul, not God, bears the responsibility for its defilement (I,9). But then, replies Augustine, it
must have existed somewhere before its entry into the body, and
Victor himself denies this (II,11)./18/

This is the state of the controversy into which Augustine introduces DNOA. He records in the *Retractationes* (II,56) that he later
received a *"scripta correctionis"* from Victor. Whether the youth
repented out of conviction that he had erred or simply under the
weight of the Bishop's authority, we cannot know. Moreover, since
we lack Victor's book and are dependent on his opponent's quotation
or paraphrase of his arguments, it is often difficult to surmise how
the arguments were developed or whether Augustine represents
them fairly. However, Augustine's correspondence with Optatus
and Jerome suggests that Victor was not an isolated voice but spoke
for a number of thoughtful Christians. At least the Bishop of Hippo
considered their refutation worth his time, even though he never
did reach a conclusion on the central question. In his very last
works he still had to admit that he did not know how God bestowed
souls on human beings./19/

Title, Text, Mechanical Matters

The fact that this treatise is not always called by the same title
goes back to a difference in the ancient texts. It appears in the man-
uscripts with the title *De Natura et Origine Animae* but in the *Retractationes* is referred to as *De Anima et Eius Origine*. Although
Possidius, Augustine's biographer, catalogues the work under mis-
cellaneous treatises, it is generally included among his anti-Pelagian
writings because of the occasional references to Pelagianism and
because of its contemporaneity with the Pelagian controversy.

I have appended to the thesis my own translation of Book III
and parts of Book IV; and throughout the thesis the translation of
DNOA is always mine. It is made from the Latin text of Urba and

Zycha in CSEL, volume 60, from 1913—the same text which is
reproduced in the *Bibliothèque augustinienne* edition of 1975. I
have been guided by the 1874 English translation of Peter Holmes
appearing in The Nicene and Post-Nicene Fathers, First Series,
volume V (reissued by Eerdmans, Grand Rapids, in 1978); by the
1975 French translation by J. Plagnieux and F.-J. Thonnard in volume 22 of the BA Oeuvres de St. Augustin, for which de Veer wrote
the introduction; and by the German translation of A. Maxsein and
D. Morick in the series *Sankt Augustinus, der Lehrer der Gnade*,
volume 3, *Schriften gegen die Pelagianer* (Würzburg: Augustinus-
Verlag, 1977).

Biblical quotatiions I have usually translated directly from Augustine's Latin text, since they often do not correspond to any modern translation. Where the Septuagint and Hebrew numberings of
chapter and verse differ, I have followed the German practice of
listing both (e.g., Ps. 48/49:12). Where Augustine quotes Victor I
have used ordinary quotation marks even though some of the instances are not exact quotations but paraphrases.

In translation I have stayed very close to the Latin original,
with the result that the reader will often have to pay the price of
sorting out long sentences and putting up with a distressing number
of *fors* and *indeeds* and *furthermores*. However, I hope that a reliable and consistent relation to the Latin original and an accurate
representation of the connectives, which are after all signposts to
the progress of the argument, will compensate for a certain lack of
sprightliness. Where words must be added to make the English
intelligible, I have not hesitated to add them but have indicated my
additions by brackets.

NOTES

Introduction

/1/   Malcolm Muggeridge's series for the BBC, *A Third Testament*, included St. Augustine, as did Steve Allen's *Meeting of the Minds*.

/2/   Also known, less commonly, as *De Anima et Eius Origine*. I shall
use the better-known title and, for convenience, abbreviate it as DNOA.

/3/   The phrase actually comes from Augustine, *Ep.* 130 to Proba (CSEL 44). The letter is cited by Nicholas of Cusa in his *Apologia Doctae Ignorantiae* (Jasper Hopkins, *Nicholas of Cusa's Debate with John Wenck* [Minneapolis: Banning Press, 1981], section 13, p. 51.)

/4/   Chapter I of this study enlarges on this topic and gives sources.

/5/   See for example *Cat.Rud.* I,3,5; I,13,18–19; I,15,23; DDC IV,22,51.

/6/   *Cat.Rud.* I,2,4; I,10,14; I,12,17; DDC IV,12,27–29; IV,5,8.

/7/   In his introduction to the BA edition of DNOA, found in vol. 22 of the Oeuvres de St. Augustin (Paris: Desclée de Brouwer, 1975), pp. 273–320; and in "Origines de *De natura et origine animae* de St. Augustin," REA 19:1–2 (1973), pp. 121–157.

/8/   In BA, vol. 22, note 27, p. 756, de Veer concludes that Optatus's bishopric was probably in Mauretania Tingitana (modern Tangiers). An English translation of *Ep.* 190 appears in FOC, vol. 30, pp. 271–288.

/9/   de Veer dates Bk. I to December of 419 or January 420 (BA vol. 22, p. 288).

/10/   *De Princ.* I,8,4; III,3,6.

/11/   *Ad Orosium liber unus,* PL 42: 669–678.

/12/   See *Ep.* 165, 166, 172, 202A.

/13/   See *Ep.* 166, dated 415. He lists the choices in ch. 7; his reference to an earlier work is to *De Libero Arbitrio.*

/14/   In *Ep.* 166,27, Augustine calls the idea of transmigration of souls "revolting." However, *De Genesi ad Litteram* X considers, in relation to creationism, a sense in which souls may be thought to preexist logically or ideally.

/15/   Tertullian, *Adv. Prax.* VII,8. "Quis enim negabit Deum corpus esse?" Augustine refers to this at II,9 and IV,18 of DNOA. An explanation of Tertullian's terminology is G. C. Stead's "Divine Substance in Tertullian," JTS 14:1 (April, 1963), pp. 47–67. See my ch. 2, pp. 43–46.

/16/   "L'intention d'Augustin en abordant le livre X est donc bien d'éliminer le traducianisme." BA 49, p. 531.

/17/   See *Ep.* 166,8 for Jerome's creationism. In ch. 27 there is only passing mention of traducianism. The Catholic Church ultimately decided in favor of creationism; for a summary of the history of the debate, see Robert LaCroix, *L'origine de l'âme humaine* (Québec: L'action catholique, 1945).

/18/ There is a third, but unacceptable, possibility, the dualist notion that sin is the work of an independent malevolent force. Augustine had spent ten years under that delusion as a member of the Manichaean sect, but finally rejected its claim of "opposing powers and natures which were not created by You" (*Conf.* VIII,3) and concluded that "evil is only the privation of a good" (*Conf.* III,12).

/19/ "Nec tunc sciebam, nec nunc scio," *Retr.* I,1,3. "Me nescire confiteor," *Contra Secundam Julianum Responsionem Opus Imperfectum,* II,168. PL 45, cols. 1049–1608.

CHAPTER 1

THE RETURN TO RHETORIC

Augustine, the professor of rhetoric, inherited a long and rich oratorical tradition that had survived translation, deportation, and radical changes in politics, social structures, and religion. This chapter will examine strands of thought that particularly influenced rhetoric up to Augustine's time and will attempt to come to some conclusions about how Augustine made use of these thoughts. Cicero's influence is direct and, all modern writers agree, determinative. What Augustine knew of Plato, Aristotle, or Isocrates, however, was very little firsthand; historians are also agreed that his knowledge of Greek was sketchy/1/ and that even his reading in translation of the Greek philosophers seems to have been limited to what was included in handbooks and summaries of the time. Yet there is also no doubt that it is accurate to speak of Augustine as a Platonist./2/ The following pages are, therefore, concerned not to prove literary dependence but rather to analyze Augustine's choices of the ideas current in his time.

Augustine's account of his early life, the *Confessions*, relates not one but two conversions. The first is his conversion from rhetoric to philosophy, a step in what John Ryan calls "his personal *praeparatio evangelica*."/3/ The second, his conversion to the Catholic Church, does not come until twelve years later in the famous *Tolle lege* episode recorded in *Confessions* VIII,12,29.

Here is Augustine's account of his first conversion, occasioned by the reading of Cicero's *Hortensius*:

> Inter hos ego inbecilla tunc aetate discebam libros eloquentiae, in qua eminere cupiebam, fine damnabili et ventoso per gaudia vanitatis humanae; et usitate iam discendi ordine perveneram in librum cuiusdam Ciceronis, cuius linguam fere omnes mirantur, pectus non ita. Sed liber ille ipsius exhortationem continet ad philosophiam et vocatur Hortensius. Ille vero liber mutavit affectum meum, et ad te

ipsum, domine, mutavit preces meas, et vota ac desideria
mea fecit alia. Viluit mihi repente omnis vana spes, et inmortalitatem sapientiae concupiscebam aestu cordis incre-
dibili, et surgere coeperam, ut ad te redirem. Non enim ad
acuendam linguam, quod videbar emere maternis merce-
dibus, . . . neque mihi locutionem, sed quod loquebatur
persuaserat./4/
    Quomodo ardebam, deus meus, quomodo ardebam re-
volare a terrenis ad te. . . . Amor autem sapientiae nomen
graecum habet philosophiam, quo me accendebant illae lit-
terae.

(Among such associates of my callow youth I studied the
treatises on eloquence, in which I desired to shine, for a
damnable and inflated purpose, directed towards empty
human joys. In the ordinary course of study I came upon a
book by a certain Cicero, whose tongue almost all men admire but not his heart. This work contains his exhortation
to philosophy and is called *Hortensius*. This book changed
my affections. It turned my prayers to you, Lord, and
caused me to have different purposes and desires. All my
vain hopes forthwith became worthless to me, and with in-
credible ardor of heart I desired undying wisdom. I began
to rise up, so that I might return to you. I did not use that
book to sharpen my tongue: that I seemed to purchase with
the money my mother gave to me. . . . Nor did it impress
me by its way of speaking but rather by what it spoke.
    How I burned, O my God, how I burned with desire
to fly away from earthly things and upwards to you. . . .
Love of wisdom has the name philosophy in Greek, and
that book set me on fire for it.

Augustine's rhetorical career accumulates a whole set of pejorative
terms: *"damnabili et ventoso," "gaudia vanitatis humanae," "vana
spes," "ad acuendam linguam," "terrenis."* In contrast to these, philosophy offers *"inmortalitatem sapientiae."* Eloquence is a commod-
ity that money can buy; true wisdom waits on divine inspiration.
With the cool description *"cuiusdam Ciceronis,"* Augustine disso-
ciates himself from the principal representative of the rhetorical
tradition of Roman education concerned with externals, the tongue
but not the heart./5/
    Such a negative view of rhetoric is not a distinctively Christian
opinion (although one can understand why, in light of the Scriptural
condemnations of words without actions, Christians would be critical of "empty rhetoric"); Marcus Aurelius, for example, in *Meditations* I,7 classes rhetoric with "frippery of speech" and in I,17 gives

thanks that "when I had an inclination to philosophy, I did not fall into the hands of any sophist." Furthermore, although the *Hortensius* is now lost to us, the fragments preserved indicate that the dialogue is Cicero's own turning away from rhetoric in favor of philosophy./6/ The republic, and therefore the political power of rhetoricians to guide the state, had just ended with the ascendancy of Julius Caesar, and along with the dashing of Cicero's political hopes had come the personal tragedy of Tullia's loss.

Plainly, then, both Christians and pagans inherited the old debate, so evident in Plato, between rhetoric and philosophy. For Plato, rhetoric is inferior because its material is the world of becoming and passing away (τὰ γιγνόμενα), while philosophy deals with what is (τὸ ὄν). Rhetoric belongs to the world of opinion (δόξα) and appearances, whereas philosophy belongs to a world of true knowledge (ἐπιστήμη) and reality. Plato shows his unfriendliness toward rhetoric most clearly in two dialogues, the *Phaedrus* and the *Gorgias*. In one of the few straight answers Socrates ever gives an opponent, he tells Polus and Gorgias that rhetoric is a "kind of routine" (τριβή) and "part of an activity that is not very reputable."/7/ It acts on the soul as cookery acts on the body, giving the *appearance* of contributing to knowledge or health but in fact not doing any real good. In the *Theaetetus* Plato even acknowledged that the philosopher will look foolish to ordinary people occupied in the world of affairs.

Plato did, however, grant that there was a good sort of rhetoric, that it was possible for a speaker to be concerned with ἐπιστήμη and not mere δόξα. This sort of speaking is dialectic, and Socrates' incessant questioning exemplifies that art./8/ Clearly dialectic too has to do with persuasion—Plato gives it the name ψυχαγωγία in *Pheadrus* 271d—so it is not the *process* of persuasion that he objects to; his quarrel is with the *aim* of that persuasion, whether it strives to get at the truth of things or simply to look good. He complains, " In the law courts nobody cares a rap for the truth about these matters but only about what is plausible."/9/

Aristotle developed his rhetorical theories along the lines of Plato's thought, giving special attention to "the interplay of reason and emotion in discourse."/10/ But because he started from different metaphysical and epistemological assumptions as to the value of δόξα and of studying τὰ γιγνόμενα, he distinguished rhetoric from dialectic not, as Plato had done, to disapprove of one and approve of the other, but to examine the legitimate uses of each.

> Aristotle acknowledges that there is an epistemology of the
> probable, namely, that the mind can know and use the
> probable as well as the unconditional in its attempt to
> understand the world of reality./11/

In Aristotle, "rhetoric" applies particularly to the presentation of
practical questions to an audience rather than one-to-one philosophical debate about speculative questions./12/

From Aristotle's systematization of rhetoric came the following
distinctions, which passed into the later common rhetorical theory
influencing Christian rhetoric:/13/

1) The division of rhetoric into judicial, deliberative, and epideictic.
2) The relationship of *ethos, pathos,* and *logos:* how the character of the speaker, the disposition of the audience, and
   the form of the arguments interact.
3) The five parts in composing a speech: invention, arrangement, style, memory, and delivery.
4) Emphasis on clarity; recognition of correctness, ornamen-
   tation, and propriety as virtues of style.
5) Different styles of speaking appropriate to different subject
   matter (although it was apparently Theophrastus, after Aristotle, who defined specifically the plain, middle, and
   grand styles).
6) The theory of "topics" or types of argumentation.
7) The view that rhetoric is neutral, not intrinsically good or
   bad.

Plato's hostility toward rhetoric was directed at the sophists,
those who claimed to be able to impart all the knowledge one
needed to make a successful life. Isocrates represents the rhetorician's point of view as over against Plato's. Not that he disparages
philosophy, but to him philosophy means practical wisdom, including a cultivation of the art of speaking well. He does not condemn
rhetoric as Plato does but regards it as neutral—the attitude also
adopted by Aristotle, Cicero, Quintilian, and Augustine. Cato's Roman formula of the *vir bonus dicendi peritus* holds the spirit of
Isocrates' teaching. Whereas Plato's dialectic required a live dialogue between pupil and philosopher, Isocrates' speeches were
published as written works, not delivered as orations./14/

Still another difference appears in the attitude toward political
action: Socrates' questioning about the meaning of justice, virtue,
etc., has in view the health of the *polis,* and his death in obedience
to the laws of Athens shows his absolute respect for the city's deci-

sion. Yet Socrates is also clearly the man whom the *polis* cannot tolerate, for he shows his independence of its customary ways of doing things. Ultimately his refusal to accept the conventions of courtroom rhetoric results in the death sentence. For Isocrates and the sophists one imagines that getting executed would point to an egregious failure of philosophy to accomplish anything. Isocrates, on the other hand, set out a pan-Hellenic ideal which strongly influenced the direction of Greek and Roman education. Socrates' philosophy is at odds with the state; Isocrates' knows how to get along with it.

George Kennedy considers that Aristotle's further development in Plato's thought on rhetoric might, if better known, have healed the breach between Plato and the rhetoricians of Isocrates' school.

> The major tragedy in the general neglect of Aristotle's *Rhetoric* is probably the fact that until the twentieth century it failed to play the role of which it is capable in mediating between philosophy and technical or sophistic rhetoric. The quarrel between rhetoric and philosophy was taken up in Hellenistic times in much the form seen in Plato's *Gorgias*, and despite the efforts of Cicero in *De Oratore*, has repeatedly exasperated partisans on both sides./15/

For Cicero

> this distinction between philosophy and rhetoric was "absurd, useless and objectionable, because there is no distinction between one who learns to know and one who learns to speak" (*De Orat.* III,16,61). Cicero considered the distinction absurd on account of the inseparable unity between "*res*" and "*verba*," content and form, thinking and speaking./16/

> Cicero's ideal was to unite the existence of a philosopher, statesman and orator in one man, thus striving for a synthesis of philosophy, politics, and rhetoric./17/

Cicero has received less respect as an original thinker than as a transmitter of Greek ideas to Rome, but his synthesis had the most profound effect on Augustine and so on Western thought. Ironically the work which became his most famous bequest to future rhetoricians was *De Inventione*, which was written in his youth, based on the system he had learned at school, and superseded by the far more sophisticated works of his maturity, *De Oratore, Brutus*, and the *Orator*. The early treatise expressed the necessity of combining wisdom and eloquence (i.e., philosophy and rhetoric) toward the

Roman ideal of political development, in contrast to the Greek withdrawal of philosophers from political action. He maintained the division of rhetoric into judicial, deliberative, and epideictic; defined topics; gave instructions for putting together a speech in its five parts (as mentioned above under Aristotle's system); and gave some history of rhetoric.

But "his greatest legacy is his own oratory, which is closely associated with his vision of the orator as set forth in *De Oratore*."/18/ That vision combines rhetorical theory from the Platonic and Aristotelian writings with the Isocratean sophistic tradition, and because Cicero's interest does not stop with rhetoric but extends to examining the philosophical debates of the schools, he becomes the source of all subsequent Western thought not only about rhetoric but about its relation to philosophy. The medieval humanistic traditions all go back to Cicero. Joseph Mazzeo enumerates them thus:/19/

1) the strictly literary tradition of Cicero and Quintilian,
2) the fusion of Aristotle's logic with Cicero's writing on definitions and principles,
3) the theological and philosophical tradition, through Augustine, which blended Platonism with Cicero.

Kennedy claims only one real rhetorical innovation for Cicero: /20/ the concept of the *officia oratoris*, that the orator tries to teach, to please, and to move to action. This triad—*docere, placere* (or *delectare*), *movere* (or *flectere*)—has an important place in Augustine's *De Doctrina Christiana* IV. Two other points of Cicero's become central to Augustine's thought also:

1) *res* and *verba*, matter and words, which in Cicero refers to the distinction between an action and what is said about it. But it is certainly susceptible of being understood as a much deeper distinction between philosophy and rhetoric, between meaning and expression, or between reality and (mere) images. This is, in fact, what Augustine makes of it.

2) *ratio* and *auctoritas* in Cicero's *Academica* and *Republic* indicate types of proof: what can be seen by reason and what is testified to by witnesses. The former is superior if one is arguing in the courtroom. For Augustine *auctoritas* is the Scriptural witness that testifies to what *ratio* cannot figure out on its own. But the two are complementary ways of getting at the truth.

Cicero did broaden the meaning of these pairs beyond their simple courtroom application, but they were invested with enormous significance once they mingled with Judaeo-Christian ideas. Writers have differed considerably in their assessment of Augustine's debt to Cicero. The studies of Eskridge, Barry, and Haggendahl/21/ have focused particularly on the verbal similarities in the rhetorical works of the two authors. (Augustine makes no bones about using the terminology of his Roman education in *De Doctrina Christiana* and admitting its usefulness, though he does not name Cicero.) Baldwin credits Augustine with "recovering the true ancient rhetoric."/22/ Marrou and Testard grant that Cicero is the general model for Augustine in far more than rhetoric./23/ Other critics protest that, while the terminology is unquestionably Ciceronian, the philosophical basis of the terms has been so altered that Augustine is the father of "a uniquely Christian conception of the art of rhetoric."/24/

But if rhetorical theory depends on philosophical assumptions, as the literature on rhetoric seems to agree, then one should return again to the conversion account with which this chapter began, to see what Augustine's philosophical assumptions were during this period of turning toward the Church. *Confessions* III is reaching back 25 years to Augustine's reading of the *Hortensius*,/25/ and successive events have led him to interpret the book's effect as decisive. Its message was that consolation and wisdom lay in philosophy, not in "mingling and involvement . . . in the faults and errors of men."/26/ In the later *De Trinitate* (finished around 417) Augustine preserves some longer fragments of the book, including the sentence "una igitur essemus beati cognitione naturae et scientia . . . ," Which he interprets as: "The good soul is blessed through nothing else but the cognizance and knowledge, which is contemplation, of that Nature which is supremely good and lovable," viz., God./27/ Cicero does not, in these fragments of the *Hortensius* which we possess, speak as a sceptic of the New Academy, nor did Augustine read him that way. Augustine was so sure of Cicero's firm belief in a divine wisdom that in his early writings, he represented Cicero as a Platonist who was hiding his true opinions./28/

> À Cassiciacum, Augustin distingue le Cicéron des belles phrases, qu'il n'apprécie guère, du Cicéron véritable qui défend la doctrine de Platon./29/

At age 19, Augustine had not yet come across the "*libri platon-*

ici," but the desire for wisdom had been kindled and his conversion had begun.

It is interesting to note where the term "conversion" is used by Plato. In *Republic* VII 518d–520, there are several occurrences of στρέφω compounds to picture the turning away from the mere images of the cave to reality. Nock mentions that Christians later picked up from this Platonic usage the word ἐπιστροφή as a synonym for the New Testament μετάνοια./30/ The picture of conversion as the turning away from temporal images having to do with probability or plausibility to eternal realities (or substitute: from τὰ γιγνόμενα to τὸ ὄν, from δόξα to ἐπιστήμη fits well with Augustine's description of his conversion from rhetoric to philosophy in *Confessions* III. Nor does the Platonic likeness end here. καταβατέον οὖν: the one who has seen reality is bound by responsibility to the community to go back down into the cave, where he will better manage the affairs of the *polis* than one with no such grasp of reality. Augustine too was to be called back from his philosophic retreat to the affairs of the Christian community—but not merely so that the Church might be more efficiently or justly governed. Rather he would find himself drawn into a kind of ψυχαγωγία.

Between the two conversion stories—*Hortensius* and the "*tolle lege*" event—lie 13 years in pursuit of wisdom. The fact that Augustine remained a student and teacher of rhetoric for another 10 years after supposedly rejecting it reflects the circumstances of educational life:

> There was no choice for the philosophical opposition within the educational system of antiquity, but to work within the framework of the rhetorical schools: so complete had the triumph of Isocrates over Plato long since become./31/

Augustine remained a rhetor but embraced at the same time a serious study of the liberal arts (recommended by Cicero as necessary training for the competent orator). His search for wisdom led him to become a Manichee, but ironically it was his grasp of the most important philosophical issues which drove him back out of that sect.

One might see those 14 years between the reading of the *Hortensius* (in 373) and Augustine's baptism (387) as the gradual triumph of Plato over Isocrates,/32/ of philosophy over rhetoric, love of wisdom over practical success. Manichaeism looked like the philosopher's way at first. When it proved illusory, Augustine briefly considered the claims of the New Academy (in 384), but scepticism also left him unsatisfied. Then the *libri platonici* came into his hands,/33/ and the same flash of illumination that the *Hortensius* had produced years earlier struck again. He was ripe for that second conversion—to the Catholic faith—recorded in *Confessions* VIII,12.

If the first conversion had turned him from "empty words" to a search for content within his profession, the second marked an external break, through his retirement from his teaching post. Now, it seemed, he would embrace the traditional life of the philosopher, for his resignation enabled him to move to the countryside to pursue that *otium* praised by philosophers, *in otio deificare*, as he put it in a letter to a friend./34/ Obviously Augustine's conversion was not entirely a result of reading "pagan" authors. His mother's faith aroused hope in him of finding wisdom in the Scriptures of the Church. "I accordingly decided to turn my mind to the Holy Scriptures and to see what they were like."/35/ He tells us that their obscurity and his rhetor's pride drove him away again. Though he had decided that *eloquentia* should be secondary, such a total lack of it put him off. Their apparent barbarism at first seemed to allow him no other way of understanding them than by virtually eliminating the Old Testament from consideration as the Marcionites had earlier done and as now the Manichaeans were doing. His very skill as a user of words rendered him unable to cope with language that operated with the bare aim of telling something without any apparent regard to the form of the telling. Part of his conversion from rhetoric had to be lessons in a new way of reading. This instruction he finally obtained in Milan.

> It was finally from the eminent scholar Ambrose of Milan that he learned how to read Scripture, grasping its "spiritual meaning" and "inner truth." Augustine was evidently deeply impressed by Ambrose, remarking that the bishop, discarding convention, did not read aloud (*Conf.*VI,3,3). This new manner of reading, by which one can be ever mindful of the real meaning, is an extremely important aspect of the change which Augustine underwent. In the same way as famous writers are influential because of a new style of writing which they introduced, outstanding thinkers are often impressive because they learnt to read in a new way./36/

Although Ambrose's ability to read silently was not "new" in an absolute sense,/37/ apparently it was new to Augustine and stuck in his memory. Ijsseling makes an interesting connection between Ambrose's novel behavior and his way, also new to Augustine, of understanding Scripture's "inner meaning." In classical rhetoric, oral and written language followed essentially the same rules,/38/ as, for example, in the orations of Isocrates. But Scripture's often crude text seemed to break that link and to disregard altogether the customary organizations of sound and structure that characterized the literature that Augustine had hitherto encountered in his training. At the end of his career, when Augustine returned to *De Doctrina Christiana* to write its last section, he was able to work out a connection between classical and Biblical rhetoric in some respects. In Book IV he illustrates Cicero's *officia*—to instruct, to please, and to persuade/39/—by examples from Scripture, and then gives examples from the Apostle Paul of the corresponding three styles of speaking—the plain, the moderate, and the grand./40/ But before he could find that connection, he had to be able to dissociate sense from sound, to acknowledge that words could be powerful or convey truth without necessarily sounding good.

When Augustine first looked at Scripture (after the *Hortensius* episode, *Conf.* III,5,9), it was, as he tells us, because he wished to put a *name* to the wisdom commended by Cicero, and he thought that Christ's name might fill the gap. But he was not prepared for the rough clothing in which he there found Christ: "It seemed to me unworthy of comparison with the nobility of Cicero's writings. My swelling pride turned away from its humble style."/41/ He had run up against a paradox central to Christianity: that "God chose what is foolish in the world to shame the wise, God chose what is weak in the world to shame the strong."/42/ Just as his human pride balked at the humiliation of baptism,/43/ his professional pride shrank from associating himself with such inelegance of language.

A necessary element in his "new way of reading" was to recognize *humilitas* as a virtue, both in the search for true wisdom and in the language of Scripture and preaching. The term had been used before by the Stoics and by Cicero and Quintilian to refer to the plain style. But in non-Christian literature the word "*humilitas*," if referring to personal qualities, usually connoted meanness. Christians, however, linked the stylistic virtue of *humilitas* to the personal virtue of Christ in the Incarnation (Phil.2:7)./44/ And although Augustine's respect for the Platonists never wavered (he always considered them the most "like us" of any adherents of the current philosophies),/45/ it was in this one quality that he found them lacking. When Augustine thinks back on how he read the "books of the Platonists,"/46/ he fastens on the Incarnation as the missing element. Plotinus has plenty to say about the sublimity of God but nothing about God's condescension. By the time the Bishop writes *City of God*, Book X, approximately 18 years later, his criticism is directed precisely to this one point: denial of the Incarnation arises from *superbia*. This is really the only point at which Augustine blames the Platonic philosophers, for only their pride is said to prevent them from considering Christian claims seriously.

> Humility was the necessary condition for submission to this truth; and it is no easy task to persuade the proud necks of you philosophers to accept this yoke. . . . The only reason [that the teachings of Christianity seem incredible] is that Christ is humble and you are proud./47/

If the Incarnation is the essential revelation of God's nature that cannot be discovered even by the philosophers most "like us," then it becomes entirely credible that this God should choose also a different sort of language than what "the wise" would expect./48/ The apparent barbarism of Scripture is not evidence of its writers' ignorance but of God's choosing "what is weak in the world to shame the strong." Thus the humble style of Scripture could become in Augustine's eyes a positive virtue.

The glorification of *humilitas* contradicted the elitism of the Roman rhetorical education system. The spiritual strength and insight of Monica reminded Augustine constantly that wisdom was not a matter of education. His approving comments on the quick comprehension of his listeners dot his sermons, illustrating his appreciation of the common wisdom possessed by ordinary folk. And in *De Doctrina Christiana* (IV,29,62) he encourages preachers/teachers to learn the speeches of more eloquent men by heart if they have not the natural facility or formal education to persuade by their own speeches.

To the two elements of a "new way of reading" that Ambrose offered to Augustine—viz. dissociating sense from sound and appreciation for *sermo humilis*—one must add a third: the allegorical method. Looking for hidden meanings in bare or obscure words was not, in fact, new territory for a product of Roman education. The rejection by the philosophers of the Homeric accounts of divine immorality had fostered allegorical interpretation on the theory that since the literal meaning seemed blasphemous or ridiculous, a fig-

urative meaning must lie behind it./49/ Augustine's principle, after
long consideration of the method was this:

> Whatever appears in the divine word that does not literally
> pertain to virtuous behaviour or to the truth of faith, you
> must take to be figurative. . . . Scripture teaches nothing
> but charity. . . . /50/

Once the problem of crudity had been gotten over, there was
no difficulty with the idea of taking a written text seriously or of
studying it in the minutest detail, as Augustine would have done
for years with the texts of Vergil and Homer. In fact it has been
pointed out that one of the (to us) maddening habits of patristic
exegesis—viz., the steadfast refusal to see the forest for the trees,
the tendency to become lost in detail with no eye to context—is a
perfectly logical result of the training of the *grammaticus*./51/
     It is hardly surprising that Augustine found the rhetorical con-
ventions of Scripture strange.

> Augustine's intellectual furniture at the time of his conver-
> sion, let us remember, was that of classical philosophy. He
> knew nothing of Christian theology except the little he
> might have gleaned from Ambrose's sermons. He was just
> as much at the "beginnings" of theological reflection as,
> say, Justin Martyr or Clement of Alexandria long before
> him./52/

With Ambrose's preaching behind him, he was able to return,
around the time of his baptism, to the study of Scripture with some
understanding and with the necessary humility. He went to Paul
just after his readings in the *"libri platonici"* and again contrasted
the pride of the philosophers with the humility of Scriptures./53/
But when Ambrose himself urged him to read Isaiah, he had to give
up./54/ The change in his reading becomes evident, however, between his baptism (387) and 391 when he was ordained. Finaert
notes that by that time his classical allusions had given way almost
entirely to Biblical ones and his prose was permeated with Scriptural language./55/
     What conventions of Biblical rhetoric, apart from those already
mentioned, gave it an alien sound to an educated Roman reader?
Amos Wilder goes so far as to say

> The whole compendium of Israel's literature is built upon
> peculiar rhetorics that find no place in the textbooks of Ar-
> istotle or Quintilian./56/

Speaking and hearing are given the highest position of trustworthiness, higher than seeing: "The faith identifies itself fundamentally with the arts of hearing as against those of sight and touch."/57/ The gods of Israel's enemies are visible, but they are "dumb idols." Therefore, words have great significance. "God speaks and it is done,"/58/ and it is the word of God which creates and which stands forever./59/ This creative word of God is synonymous in the Hebrew Biblical tradition with God's action; in the New Testament Luke's use of ῥῆμα, in those passages where he is most closely imitating the Old Testament, carries the meaning of what is already done or what is promised and fulfilled./60/

The high opinion of words extends to the written word: γέγραπται, "It is written," is the last word to many arguments and pronouncements in Scripture./61/ By contrast, Plato deplores the effect of writing on people's memories (*Phaedrus* 274d–275b), declares that writing, like painting, is merely "a kind of image" (276a), and in Letter VII (341b-e) announces the futility of writing as a way of bringing people to truth./62/ The contrast cannot be pressed too hard, however; Scripture too distinguishes spirit from letter, the intent of the command from its mere formulation. On the other side, Plato's dialogues were written down and published.

The highest honor paid to words in the Christian tradition is that which the Gospel of John gives—that "the Word" is in John's prologue the name of Christ. John believes that the Word which God spoke at creation is to be identified with this human historical personage, Jesus. To be sure, it is not John's invention to connect λόγος with the intelligible order of the universe or with the mediating principle between God and the world./63/ But John claims that λόγος is incarnate in a historical person: "the Word became flesh."/64/

Kennedy and Wilder both point out that whereas Christian rhetoric is essentially proclamation, classical rhetoric is persuasion. /65/ It is hard to make a very clear-cut distinction here. Preaching is indeed proclamation, and there is a curious sense in which the speaker vanishes from consideration: the power to convert lies in God or in the Holy Spirit, not in the preacher's skill. Yet there is also much of persuasion in Christian rhetoric: the paranetic sections of Paul's epistles, the exhortations to right living incumbent upon the faithful, Augustine's confrontation with heretics, to give some examples. And on the other side, there is a sense of the limit to pure persuasion in the classical authors:

> [Rhetoric] does not effect persuasion as some of the tech-
> nographers said, nor does it, as far as Aristotle is concerned,
> make persuasion in the same sense as the artist makes his
> object. Rather it creates an attitude in another's mind, a
> sense of the reasonableness of the position proposed,
> whereby the auditor may make his own decision. . . . The
> auditor must step forward to accept or reject, to make his
> particular judgment to act or not to act./66/

One difference frequently mentioned between Christian and classical rhetoric, that classical has its basis in the plausible or probable, Christian in the truth, seems to ignore one obvious reason for the difference, viz. that classical writers on rhetorical theory are dealing with the necessities of the courtroom and the public assembly and not with questions of religious import./67/ The old Platonic distinction between τὸ ὄν and τὰ γιγνόμενα is operating again, and it is true that Christian orators claim to have found out more about just what τὸ ὄν is. But they are just as ready to argue on the basis of plausibility when circumstances demand, for example, to make a plausible case for Christianity to their contemporaries: Justin Martyr, Clement of Alexandria, and even the supposedly anti-intellectual Tertullian are examples of Christians asserting to their cultured despisers that there is nothing intrinsically outlandish about the Christian message. *De Natura et Origine Animae* itself represents an argument where "the truth" is unobtainable. Augustine proves that neither human reason nor the authority of Scripture offers an irrefutable answer to the problem of the soul's origin. Since he has no wish to defend one or the other of the plausible alternatives, he turns his persuasive powers on Vincentius Victor to urge him to consider the limits of knowledge more closely.

Persuasion/proclamation, reason/authority, the plausible/the truth—do these pairs correspond in any way? Does Christian rhetoric belong to one side or the other in any of the pairs? I have already mentioned (p. 18 above) Augustine's transformation of Cicero's *ratio/auctoritas* distinction into a distinction between human reason and Scriptural authority. Augustine makes copious appeals to both—in *De Natura et Origine Animae*, as Chapter 2 will show, as well as in his sermons. I would prefer, therefore, to illustrate Christian rhetoric by means of the following pairs and to argue that both sides figure in the construction of Christian preaching and apology.

Platonic attention to τὸ ὄν	Aristotelian-Ciceronian-sophistic attention to τὰ γιγνόμενα
the truth	the plausible
Scripture as *auctoritas*	human reason as *ratio*
proclamation of divine action	persuasion to human action

These pairs take into consideration the special characteristics of Christian rhetoric, noted in the previous four pages, without denying that the categories of classical rhetoric are still operative./68/ Obviously I am not arguing that Plato somehow supports the quoting of Scriptural authority but that Augustine understands Scripture as Word of God and therefore as a given, a part of τὸ ὄν.

Augustine's starting point, in fact, for thinking about the meaning of Word of God, of Scripture, and of words in general is Platonism. It was the Platonists who had given him a solution to materialism,/69/ and he looked to them also in the matter of language. The theory of Forms—the theory that the visible world is an image of the exemplar-world of Ideas—Augustine accepted. But he followed the Neoplatonist and Christian development, which located the Ideas in the mind of God./70/ His "theory of signs" assumed a similar relationship between words and their meaning: viz., that words, *verba*, are images or symbols of the things, *res*, which they represent./71/ Likewise, a spoken word is an external representation of a (truer) "inner word." In Augustine's early writings the theory resulted in a distrust of words. For example, in *De Genesi contra Manichaeos* (of 388) he implies (II,32) that since the Fall thoughts can be concealed, whereas they were utterly transparent before and needed no words. Augustine was "a contemplative in the austere tradition of Plotinus. He came near to regarding speech itself as a falling away of the soul from its inner act of contemplation."/72/ It was indicative of man's fallen state that he was forced "to work with the opacities of speech, gesture, and symbol. . . ."/73/ This view is entirely consistent with Augustine's perception of his conversion as turning from rhetoric to philosophy, from the study of empty words to reality, *verba* to *res*.

The outcome of the theory of signs in *De Magistro* is that teaching is impossible. The Platonic *anamnesis* theory underlies Augustine's concept of the teacher as one who merely reminds of what the soul must grasp through illumination from the divine Teacher. One can see how preaching as proclamation could be reconciled rather easily with the Platonic idea that teaching is a species of reminding. In Christian thinking the teacher/preacher points toward the truth, but it is God who must reveal it to the soul of the listener; in Plato the rational soul is led through the "midwifery" of the dialectician to perceive the truth.

A little later, after he had had more experience with teaching the unlettered, Augustine still admitted his frustration with the intractability of words:

> For my part, I am nearly always dissatisfied with my discourse. For I am desirous of something better, which I often inwardly enjoy before I begin to unfold my thought in spoken words; but when I find that my powers of expression come short of my knowledge of the subject, I am sorely disappointed that my tongue has not been able to answer the demands of my mind. For I desire my hearer to understand all that I understand; and I feel that I am not speaking in such a manner as to effect that. This is so chiefly because intuition floods the mind, as it were, with a sudden flash of light, while the expression of it in speech is a slow, drawn-out, and far different process, and while speech is being formed, intellectual apprehension has already hidden itself in its secret recesses./74/

His opinion has not changed 15 years later:

> What am I doing even now while I speak? I am pouring a clatter of words into your ears. What is that that I say or that I speak, unless he that is within reveal it?/75/

The sense of the inadequacy of words reaches a point which perhaps puts Augustine in the company of the mystics. The inner conversation with God "must ultimately become speechless."/76/

> True rhetoric culminates in silence, in which the mind is in immediate contact with reality. . . . For St. Augustine all dialectic, true rhetoric, and thought itself were but attempts to reascend to that silence from which the world fell into the perpetual clamor of life as fallen men know it./77/

One more peculiarity of Augustine's thinking on rhetoric deserves mention in this section because of its Platonic connections. Augustine is much interested in the question of time,/78/ and to a surprising degree his discussion of the creating Word of God is bound up with his discussion of time. Spoken words take place in

time and have a beginning, middle, and end./79/ By contrast the
Word of God is from eternity, not uttered in time. It is then a measure of God's condescension that the Word should become flesh,
that is, should consent to the bondage of time. The human life of
Christ is like our human words, having beginning, middle, and end,
as a concession to our understanding. So is the Genesis account of
creation:/80/ the recorded six days of creation are merely to aid our
understanding of God's act which took place "simul."/81/ So is the
sequence of prophecy and fulfillment, words coming true in time;
we see their fulfillment and so understand them.

Human words, then, reveal to us in time that which in God is
immutable and not bound by time. Thus, words are *signa* or *sacra-
menta* or images of the timeless. In this regard Plato's concept of
time as the moving image of eternity comes to mind. /82/

Thus within both the Platonic and the Christian traditions one
finds an ambivalence towards speech: on the one hand speech can
represent the falling away from pure thought into an inferior realm
of mere images and distractions, but on the other it possesses the
dignity which images have by virtue of their participation in the
truth. In Augustine's early career the conversion away from rhetoric
and the preoccupation with the soul's relation to God point to a
disillusionment with words and speaking. But "it was to be followed
by more profound considerations of the role of rhetoric in Christian
knowledge."/83/ Reference has already been made to Augustine's
interest in the psychology of teaching in *De Catechizandis Rudibus*.
His *Contra Cresconium* dates from around the same period (406)
and defends the legitimacy, or rather the necessity, of Christian eloquence. From these writings and *De Doctrina Christiana* (which
spanned 30 years in its composition but did not receive its final form
until 427, close to the end of his life), it is clear that Augustine came
to acknowledge the positive importance of words, indeed the Christian obligation to use them skillfully. But the ideal which must in-
form their use and underlie all eloquence is the peculiarly Christian
one of *caritas*./84/ This is the central virtue placed over against pagan and heretical *superbia*; and it explains Augustine's objections in
DNOA to Vincentius Victor's rhetoric.

James Murphy connects this rhetorical ideal of *caritas* with Aristotle's *ethos* principle—the personal character of the speaker as
he projects it in his speech:

> Augustine's concern is to make a human match between the
> didactic intent of the catechizer—the speaker—and the

learning capacity of what he calls the "hearer". . . . Only
Christian love (*caritas*) can supply this interconnection.
This is in some ways a more sophisticated concept than that
of Aristotle's *ethos*, because it posits the innate humanity of
both speaker and audience member./85/

Again this change of basis, as with the truth-vs.-plausibility contrast, is not a repudiation of classical rhetoric so much as an adaptation to new purposes. Now the burning issue was the proclamation of God's love by means of the words/signs that God provided,
the same love, Augustine says, that must operate between speaker
and listener.

The conviction that salvation hung in the balance added particular urgency to Christian rhetoric—a conviction which led Augustine to elevate clarity and immediacy to a high position:

qui utrumque non potest, dicat sapienter, quod non dicit
eloquenter, potius quam dicat eloquenter, quod dicit insi-
pienter.

(He who cannot do both should say wisely what he cannot
say eloquently rather than say eloquently what he says fool-
ishly.)/86/

Cicero says much the same thing in *De Oratore* III,35,43:

Quorum si alterum sit optandum, malim equidem indiser-
tam prudentiam quam stultitiam loquacem,

but the choice for him is hypothetical. Augustine faced the practical
difficulty of training relatively uneducated men to teach, forcing
him into some of the redefinitions of classical theory that I have
mentioned. Brown's statement may perhaps exaggerate the depar-
tures from classical tradition, but at least it recognizes the changed
circumstances:

The huge pressure built up by the need to communicate
will do nothing less than sweep away the elaborate scaffold-
ing of ancient rhetoric. For, as Augustine came to see it at
the end of his life, rhetoric had consisted of polishing an
end-product, the speech itself, according to elaborate and
highly self-conscious rules. It ignored the basic problem of
communication. . . . Immediacy was Augustine's new criterion./87/

Does Augustine achieve clarity and immediacy? It must have
been easy to fall back into the old habit of ornateness for its own

sake./88/ I will point out in the fifth chapter some of the places
where Augustine appears to indulge in eristic. Yet Marrou reminds
his readers that the standards of clarity are different in our own
time, and what seem to us obfuscations are often Augustine's device
for attracting and holding his listeners./89/ The habit of looking for
obscure meanings in Scripture sometimes caused Augustine to ignore what looks, to our eyes, like the obvious intent of the writer.
In many of his exegetical writings and sermons Augustine plays
"une sorte de jeu divin."/90/ One is astonished, for example, to discover what Augustine considers the "literal" sense of Genesis according to his title *De Genesi ad Litteram*. But again our standard
of clarity may assume a sort of "literal" interpretation quite at odds
with what was appropriate or even possible to the fifth century./91/
Augustine *wants* to draw his audience into the "jeu divin" and thus
to exercise their minds to ready them for the search for wisdom
(*"exercitatio animi"*)./92/ Furthermore he is quite aware of the part
that pleasure (*delectare* or *placere* in Cicero's three *officia* of the
orator) must play in successful persuasion. *De Catechizandis Rudibus* offers proof of his attention to delight.

> Clarity alone, if there are no other ingredients, can become
> as tiresome as a continual repetition of the same food, how-
> ever nourishing, and so a certain charm, *suavitas*, is indis-
> pensable. Even the prestige of sheer rhetorical ability plays
> a certain part, and for this reason it is a good thing for a
> Christian speaker now and then to show people that he can
> do that sort of thing as well as the next man. . . . /93/

For example, Augustine gave as good as he got from Vincentius
Victor, and Chapter 5 points to those passages which "show people
that he can do that sort of thing as well as the next man." *Humilitas*
may be abandoned now and then in order to please or to move one's
listeners.

Such attention to style hardly seems to harmonize with the picture, in the *Confessions*, of the young convert turning away from
"vain words" to contemplation of wisdom. Did Augustine abandon
his early search "to know God and the soul, nothing more"?/94/
That prayer came from a man living a monastic life, not from the
Bishop of Hippo. Yet in DNOA, the work of a long-time bishop,
one is struck by the undiminished passion for knowledge. The hunger has not changed, but only the circumstances have; and along
with the change in Augustine's situation has come the realization
that the prayer will not be granted in this life. Upon resigning from

his teacher's post in Milan, he had optimistically supposed that he was retiring from active life to contemplative life, from rhetoric to philosophy. Before his ordination, he uses the phrase "*in otio deificare*,"/95/ which could have come from the mouth of any pagan philosopher. But *otium* was not the privilege of a priest or bishop, and perhaps Augustine's tears as the crowd acclaimed him bishop were partly grief at the loss. Augustine did grasp a moment of contemplative vision at Ostia, as he and Monica glimpsed "the region of abundance . . . , where life is that wisdom by which all things are made," and then "turned back again to the noise of our mouths, where a word both begins and ends."/96/ (One sees again the contrast between the silence of philosophy and the inferior realm of speech and time.) But the vision is lost again.

> In all the writings of Augustine's maturity, he acknowledges that [for the soul to be lifted above the realm of change] is impossible. Happiness in this life can only mean the happiness of hope./97/

The predominant characteristic of the Christian's life is to be, as Augustine finds, not undivided contemplation but *desiderium*, the unsatisfied longing for the vision of God./98/

One more parallel may be instructive in comparing Augustine's early expectations with his later experience. The old quarrel between philosophy and rhetoric becomes in Christian terms the tension between the contemplative and the active life. The philosopher's *otium* would have been for Augustine the contemplation of God, but "his ordination meant the abandonment of an ideal."/99/ His pursuit of the "true philosophy" from that time on was to be bound up with the active life of the Church and with the business (*neg-otium*) of persuasion and public discourse. Yet he never ceased to commend the contemplative life or to long for it. Van der Meer cites many references to Mary and Martha, Rachel and Leah, as symbols of the contemplative and the active life./100/ Book XIV of *De Trinitate* (about 414) has the title "Perfection of the Image in the Contemplation of God"—"the Image" referring to the *imago Dei* in man. And DNOA, with all its theological disputes, semantic arguments, scientific allusions, and bursts of sarcasm still reveals Augustine's obsession with "knowing God and the soul."

Augustine initially reacted against rhetoric because of his perception of its deceit. But his considered opinion late in life was that rhetoric itself is neutral, neither good nor bad, but adaptable to either sort of purpose. Anyone called to the active life of teaching and preaching had better be prepared to turn eloquence to Christian ends, since plenty of people will be ready to turn it to pernicious use./101/

One cannot say that in Augustine there is no longer any tension between rhetoric and philosophy. But just as active and contemplative are not respectively bad and good models of Christian lives but aspects of one life subjected to different demands, so rhetoric and philosophy may alternate in prominence within one life according to circumstance. To apply a favorite illustration of the early Christian writers: just as the Israelites despoiled the Egyptians of their gold,/102/ so the Christian picks whatever is valuable from pagan wisdom and carries it off for the Church's use.

NOTES

/1/   E.g. Henri-Irénée Marrou, *St. Augustin et la fin de la culture antique* (Paris: E. de Boccard, 1938), pp.28–45; Eugene TeSelle, *Augustine the Theologian* (New York: Herder and Herder, 1970), p. 254; H. Somers, "Image de Dieu. Les sources de l'exégèse augustinienne," REA 7 (1961), pp. 105–125; Pierre Courcelle, *Late Latin Writers and Their Greek Sources* (Cambridge: Harvard University Press, 1969.)

/2/   E.g. Robert O'Connell's works (see Bibliography). Etienne Gilson, *The Christian Philosophy of St. Augustine* (New York: Random House, 1960), p. 200, says "This new Christian in search of a theology he had to elaborate himself never knew any other metaphysics but that of Plotinus and the Platonists. Since this was the only technique at his disposal, he simply had to use it. . . ."

/3/   Introduction to *The Confessions of St. Augustine* (New York: Image Books, 1960), p.22. For the idea of conversion to Christianity as a conversion from rhetoric to philosophy, I have used particularly these secondary sources: Marrou, *St. Augustin et la fin . . .* , the chapter entitled "La conversion à la philosophie"; Maurice Testard, *St. Augustin et Cicéron*(Paris: Études Augustiniennes, 1958); Rosemary Ruether, Introduction to *Gregory of Nazianzus, Rhetor and Philosopher* (Oxford: Clarendon, 1969); Samuel Ijsseling, *Rhetoric and Philosophy in Conflict* (The Hague: Nijhoff, 1976); George A. Kennedy, *Classical Rhetoric and Its Christian and Secular Tradition* (Chapel Hill: University of North Carolina Press, 1980).

34 Eloquence and Ignorance

/4/   *Conf.* III,4,7–8. The translation which follows is Ryan's, p. 81.

/5/   Testard argues (pp. 242–252) that *quidam* has no pejorative connotations in this passage and adduces several other examples in Augustine of a neutral or even laudatory sense of *quidam*. John H. Taylor "St. Augustine and the *Hortensius* of Cicero," *Studies in Philology*, 60:3 (1963), p. 492, agrees with Testard, but Hagendahl finds his arguments unconvincing (*Augustine and the Latin Classics*, Göteborg: Statens Humanistiska Forskningsråd, 1967, p. 579). The ambivalence toward Cicero is striking, whether the *"cuiusdam"* is neutral or not: Cicero is both the agent of conversion and the representative of the rejected tradition.

/6/   Taylor, pp. 487–498.

/7/   *Gorgias* 462c, cf. *Phaedrus* 260e, where rhetoric is called ἄτεχνος τριβή. The sophist Gorgias is best known for defending the propositions that (1) nothing exists; (2) if it did, we could not know it; (3) if we knew it, we could not communicate this knowledge to anyone else. Guthrie (*The Greek Philosophers*[New York: Harper, 1975], p.68) considers this a parody of contemporaneous books on "The Existent." Nevertheless the second statement would make philosophy impossible; the third would make impossible dialectic and rhetoric, the only activities which Plato puts much value on. Gorgias's suggestion would certainly arouse Plato's opposition.

/8/   *Theaet*. 150b-d.

/9/   *Phaedrus* 272e.

/10/   Wm. A. Grimaldi, *Studies in the Philosophy of Aristotle's Rhetoric* (Wiesbaden: Steiner, 1972), p. 16.

/11/   Ibid., p. 16.

/12/   Kennedy, p. 66.

/13/   Ibid., pp.62–81.

/14/   Ibid., p.35. "He is the first major 'orator' who did not deliver his speeches orally. They were carefully edited, polished, and published. . . ." Oral and written literature were not in ancient times as separated as they are today (Kennedy, p. 17; p. 109). For example, several remarks in DNOA (e.g. I,35; II,1; II,23; III,3) assume that the debate will be, as it has already been, a public reading of the documents.

/15/   Ibid., p. 81.

/16/   Ijsseling, p. 35.

/17/   Ibid., p. 34.

/18/   Kennedy, p. 100.

/19/   "St. Augustine's Rhetoric of Silence," *Journal of the History of Ideas*, 23 (1962), pp. 175–196. This description, p. 175, he acknowledges with a citation from Richard McKeon, "Rhetoric in the Middle Ages," in *Critics and Criticism*, ed. R. S. Crane (Chicago, 1952), pp. 260–296.

/20/   p. 100. The innovation is perhaps more in terminology than in substance, for the three correspond in function to Aristotle's *logos*, *ethos*, and *pathos*.

/21/   James Eskridge, *The Influence of Cicero upon Augustine in the Development of his Oratorical Theory for the Training of the Ecclesiastical Orator*(Menasha, Wis.: Collegiate Press, 1912); Sr. M. Inviolata Barry, *St. Augustine the Orator*, Patristic Studies, No. 6 (Washington, D.C.: Catholic University of America, 1924); Harald Hagendahl, *Augustine and the Latin Classics* (Göteborg: Statens Humanistiska Forskningsråd, 1967).

/22/   *Medieval Rhetoric and Poetic* (New York: Macmillan, 1928), p. 52.

/23/   *St. Augustin et la fin* . . . ,pp.521–25; Testard, Introduction to *St. Augustin et Cicéron*.

/24/   Louis D. McNew, "The Relation of Cicero's Rhetoric to Augustine," *Research Studies of the State College of Washington*, 25:1 (March, 1957), pp. 5–13. Extended treatment of this view is found in Ernest Fortin, "Augustine and the Problem of Christian Rhetoric," *Augustinian Studies*, 5 (1974), pp. 85–100.

/25/   The chronology of the events in this section is found on the Chronological Table at the beginning of the dissertation.

/26/   ". . . quo minus se admiscuerint atque implicuerint hominum vitiis et erroribus. . . ." Augustine preserves more of the *Hortensius* than any other writer. This passage he quotes in *De Trin.* XIV,19,26 (PL 42, 1056–57).

/27/   *De Trin.* XIV,9,12 (PL 42, 1046), trans. Burnaby.

/28/   *Con. Acad.*, *De Beata Vita*, *De Ordine*. Cf. the study by Margaret Young Henry, *The Relation of Dogmatism and Scepticism in the Philosophical Treatises of Cicero* (Geneva, N.Y.: W.F. Humphrey, 1925): "Cicero was not a consistent doubter; while in the theoretical sphere he denied the possibility of certain knowledge, in matters touching the foundations of morality he spoke with dogmatic certainty," pp. 3–4.

/29/   Testard, p. 174.

/30/   Arthur Darby Nock, *Conversion* (Oxford: Clarendon Press, 1933), p. 179.

/31/   E. Kevane, "Augustine and Isocrates," *American Ecclesiastical Review* 149 (163), pp. 301–321. Quote, p. 309.

/32/   Kevane's terms, see n. 31.

/33/   Concerning the *libri platonici*, see Robert O'Connell, *St. Augustine's Early Theory of Man* (Cambridge: Harvard University Press, 1968), pp. 1–15. Specific parallels with the *Enneads* are examined in O'Connell's *Confessions: The Odyssey of Soul* (Cambridge: Harvard University Press, 1969).

/34/   *Ep.* 10,2.

/35/   *Conf.* III,5,9. For his early reaction to Scripture, see *Conf.* III,7,14; IV,14,24; VI,3,4–8; IX,5,13.

/36/   Ijsseling, pp.42–43.

/37/   Bernard M. Knox, "Silent Reading in Antiquity," *Greek, Roman, and Byzantine Studies*, 9:4 (1968), pp. 421–435.

/38/   On pp. 108–114 of his *Classical Rhetoric*, Kennedy discusses *letteraturizzazione*, "the repeated slippage of rhetoric into literary composition," (p. 109). See also his following chapter (7, pp. 120–160) on Judaeo-Christian rhetoric.

/39/   DDC IV,14,30.

/40/   DDC IV,20,39–44.

/41/   *Conf.* III,5,9: "Visa est mihi indigna, quam Tullianae dignitati compararem. Tumor enim meus refugiebat modum eius. . . . "

/42/   I Cor. 1:27, RSV.

/43/   He was full of wonder when the great scholar Marius Victorinus presented himself for baptism as simply as any child. *Conf.* VIII,2,3.

/44/   See Erich Auerbach "Sermo humilis" in *Literary Language and Its Public in Late Latin Antiquity and the Middle Ages*, Bollingen Series, no. 74 (New York: Pantheon, 1965), especially pp. 35–47, for the confrontation of classical rhetoric with the Christian ideal of *humilitas*.

/45/   CD VIII,9.

/46/ *Conf.* VII,9,13. Plotinus surely, possibly also Porphyry, see note 33 this chapter.

/47/ CD X,29. I have been speaking about the philosophy-rhetoric conflict hitherto as though Augustine never had anything unflattering to say about philosophy. But in this passage one finds a hint of his only pejorative use of "philosophy," a reference often linked to the NT text of Col. 2:8 (the only NT occurrence of the abstract noun): "See to it that no one makes a prey of you by philosophy and empty deceit, according to human tradition, according to the elemental spirits of the universe and not according to Christ" (RSV). The Christian suspicion of philosophy as "empty deceit" harmonized with an older Roman distrust of Greek ideas. "The teaching of rhetoric had met with initial hostility at Rome in the second and early first centuries B.C., but by the Augustan period rhetoric was entirely acclimatized throughout the Roman Empire. Unlike philosophy it seemed useful, concrete, and manly. This distrust of philosophy and acceptance of rhetoric is generally reflected in the Christian Latin writers" (Kennedy, p. 146). However Augustine usually equates philosophy with its literal meaning, "love of wisdom," or with the Christian way ("true philosophy") and seems not to have suffered a bad conscience over his friendliness to Platonism.

/48/ Auerbach, pp. 45–46. E.g., DDC II,6,7; III,12,18; IV,6,9.

/49/ *Pheadrus*, Plato's dialogue on rhetoric, has a nice example of the interpretation of sacred myths in the opening banter about Boreas and Orithyia, 229b-e.

/50/ DDC III,10,14–15.

/51/ See, e.g., Marrou, *St. Augustin et la fin* . . . p. 429; Maurice Pontet, *L'exégèse de St. Augustin prédicateur* (Paris: Aubier, 1945), p. 232.

/52/ Eugene TeSelle, *Augustine the Theologian* (New York: Herder and Herder, 1970), p. 55.

/53/ *Conf.* VII,20,26.

/54/ *Conf.* IX,5,13.

/55/ Joseph Finaert, *L'Évolution littéraire de St. Augustin* (Paris: Société d'Édition "Les Belles Lettres," 1939), p. 17.

/56/ *Early Christian Rhetoric: The Language of the Gospel* (London: SCM, 1964), p. 15. Kennedy says Wilder "probably exaggerates," p. 128.

/57/ Ibid., p.20.

/58/ Ps. 33:9, RSV.

/59/   Gen. 1; Ps. 33:6; Is. 40:8.

/60/   E.g., Lk.1:37, 1:38, 1:65, 2:15, 2:19, 2:29.

/61/   E.g., the temptation of Christ in Lk. 4:4–10. Interestingly it is the Devil who takes up the word γέγραπται the third time, perhaps grasping for the final authority to legitimize his claim.

/62/   Plato's low regard for writing is as ironic as his criticism of the poets—the master writer and poet turning his back on the art he uses. Cicero noted the discrepancy: "What impressed me most deeply about Plato in that book *Gorgias* was, that it was when making fun of orators that he himself seemed to me to be the consummate orator" (*De Orat.* I,11,47). Plato's insistence on the superiority of the spoken word has a Christian parallel in Papias's statement regarding his attempts to collect eyewitness traditions pertaining to the writing of the Gospels: "I did not suppose that information from books would help me so much as the word of a living and surviving voice." (Eusebius *Eccles. Hist.* III,39,4, trans. Kirsopp Lake, Loeb Classical Library [New York: Putnam, 1926], p. 293.) Luther's theology contrasts the efficacy of "living Word" with mere "letter."

/63/   See sources listed by A.H. Armstrong and R.A. Markus, *Christian Faith and Greek Philosophy* (London: Darton, Longman and Todd, 1960), Chapter 3, "The Word and the Ideas," pp. 16–29.

/64/   Jn. 1:14.

/65/   Kennedy, p. 127; Wilder, p. 31.

/66/   Grimaldi, p. 27.

/67/   The articles of Ernest Fortin and Louis McNew seem to be somehow blaming Cicero for not being in every way adequate to the demands of Christian rhetoric. Kennedy (pp. 120–160) appreciates the interaction of classical and Christian principles. Augustine himself recognizes this change in the material of rhetoric in DDC IV,18,35, where he quotes Cicero on the matters to which the plain, moderate, and grand styles are appropriate, noting that in Christian preaching and teaching there are no "small" matters.

/68/   It also permits agreement with a statement such as W.R. Johnson's in "Isocrates Flowering: The Rhetoric of Augustine," *Philosophy and Rhetoric* 9:4 (Fall, 1976), pp.217–231: "Augustine had Plato in his mind and heart, but he had Isocrates in his blood," p. 227. This statement recognizes the importance of both the major classical traditions.

/69/   *Conf.* VII,20,26.

/70/   Armstrong and Markus, pp. 16–17.

/71/   The theory of signs is set out in *De Mag.* and DDC, especially Book II. For its connection to Stoic logic, see R. H. Ayers, *Language, Logic, and Reason in the Church Fathers* (Hildesheim: Olms, 1979), pp. 68–75.

/72/   Peter Brown, *Augustine of Hippo* (Berkeley: University of California Press, 1967), p. 256.

/73/   Robert O'Connell, *Confessions: The Odyssey of Soul* (Cambridge: Harvard University Press, 1969), p. 155.

/74/   *Cat. Rud.* 2,3; ACW p. 15. Written between 400–405.

/75/   *Tractates on the Gospel of St. John* 26,7 (PL 35, trans. PNF 1st series, vol. 7, p. 170), written in 416–417.

/76/   Ijsseling, p. 45.

/77/   Mazzeo, pp. 187 and 192.

/78/   E.g., the famous Bk. XI discourse on time in the *Conf.* See also CD XII,4–6 and 16–21. Augustine's *De Musica* has perhaps more to do with time than it does with what a modern reader would consider to be the elements of music.

/79/   *Conf.* XI,34; *Tractates on John* 1,8 (PNF 1st Series, vol.7, p. 10.).

/80/   That interpretation is hinted at in earlier works: *Conf.* XIII,29; *De Gen. adv. Mani.* II,3 (PL 34); explicit later in *De Gen. ad Litt.* IV, chs. 33–35.

/81/   Sir. 18:1.

/82/   *Tim.* 37d.

/83/   Kennedy, p. 151. It is interesting that just recently the supposedly anti-intellectual Tertullian has been the subject of three major studies (R. H. Ayers, *op. cit.*; Timothy David Barnes, *Tertullian: A Historical and Literary Study*, Oxford, 1971; Robert Dick Sider, *Ancient Rhetoric and the Art of Tertullian*, Oxford, 1971), all concluding that far from being hostile to rhetoric, Tertullian exemplifies a reconciliation of classical and Christian ideals.

/84/   DDC I,36,40; *Cat. Rud.* I,4,8; II,26,50.

/85/   "The Metarhetoric of Plato, Augustine, and McLuhan: A Pointing Essay," *Philosophy and Rhetoric* 4:4 (1971), p. 208.

/86/   DDC IV,28,61, trans. LLA. Clarity lucidity, and immediacy are terms used by Marrou, p. 525; F. Van Der Meer, *Augustine the Bishop* (New York: Sheed and Ward, 1961), p. 408; and Brown, p. 256. DDC IV,9,23: "non curante illo qui docet, quanta eloquentia doceat, sed quanta evidentia": "The speaker should not consider the eloquence of his teaching but the clarity of it."

/87/   Brown, p. 256.

/88/   See ch. 5 below, pp. 122–123, which cites places where Augustine seems rather carried away with ornateness for its own sake. But the style of these passages might also be defended as part of the "jeu divin" which charms and thus persuades the reader.

/89/   Marrou, *Augustin et la fin* . . . , pp. 525–535.

/90/   Pontet, p. 181. Joseph Finaert, *St. Augustin rhéteur* (Paris: Société des études latines, 1939), p. 53, calls Augustine's digressions and fanciful etymologies "jeux d'esprit."

/91/   "Ad Litteram" does not, it is true, mean "literal" quite in the modern sense but rather "to the letter," i.e., proceeding line by line, word by word. But his intention in doing so, as he tells us in *Retr.* II,24, was to examine the first chapters of Genesis "non secundum allegoricas significationes, sed secundum rerum gestarum proprietatem." To a modern reader, what he considers to be "secundum rerum gestarum proprietatem" ("according to the proper historical sense," ACW) is often surprising.

/92/   Marrou, (p. 409) defends Augustine's lucidity for all his discursive style but criticizes him for the "decadence and utilitarianism" whose seeds lie in the sophistic view that the study of the liberal arts is only so much grist for the orator's mill. This uncritical and unsystematized scattering of odd bits of knowledge and *mirabilia* through one's writing becomes more common in the Middle Ages.

/93/   Van Der Meer, p. 408. See DDC IV,22,51–52; *Cat. Rud.* I,2,4.

/94/   *Solil.* 1,7, the first book Augustine wrote after his baptism, during the Cassiciacum retreat.

/95/   *Ep.* 10,2.

/96/   *Conf.*, IX,10,23.

/97/   John Burnaby, *Amor Dei* (London: Hodder and Stoughton, 1938), p. 50.

/98/   Ibid., p. 98.

/99/ Ibid., p. 50.

/100/ p. 647, n. 41.

/101/ DDC IV,2,3. It is, of course, also possible to reverse the traditional assumption of the priority of philosophy to rhetoric. See, for example, Ernesto Grassi, "Can Rhetoric Provide a New Basis for Philosophizing?" *Philosophy and Rhetoric* 11:1 (1978), pp. 1–17; and 11:2 (1978), pp. 75–95. "True wisdom, by which history develops, is the art of speech which now becomes the source of 'true' philosophy in place of the a priori deduction of the nature of reality," p. 87.

/102/ DDC II,40,60.

CHAPTER 2

"NOLI CREDERE . . .": VICTOR'S ERRORS

Three things offended Victor when he read Augustine's short work, Epistle 190, on the nature and origin of the soul: (1) that Augustine would not choose a position, when to Victor creationism seemed the clear sense of Scripture, (2) that Augustine assigned to the soul a spiritual, as opposed to a corporeal, nature, and (3) that he called the soul a spirit. Augustine had considered 2 and 3 the same point, but Victor separated them (IV,2).

Victor may have been disappointed in the Bishop's reply, for Augustine only clung more obstinately to the fence between creationism and traducianism and denied prime importance to the other two points, regarding them as arguments over terminology, not substance. His defense of his suspended judgment he reserved for Book IV, and instead of sticking to Victor's chosen territory for debate, he attacked him on eleven other points. These he considered really heretical, not simply misguided or absurd like Victor's body/soul/spirit confusion.

Before looking at the eleven errors, it is useful to understand the background to Victor's view of the soul, for his confusion in terminology is inherited, as Augustine recognizes. Victor's major source was Tertullian's *De Anima*, as one can see particularly from his picture of the soul encased in the body,/1/ and from Tertullian he inherited his notion of *corpus*. In this view, if a thing were not *corpus*, it was nothing./2/

Spanneut, in his study of Stoic influences on the Fathers,/3/ attributes Tertullian's advocacy of Stoic beliefs to the particular heresies he faced. On the one hand were critics who wished to deny the divine origin of the soul (Hermogenes for one, see *Adversus Hermogenen*) and on the other the Platonists who threatened to open a great gulf between body and soul. Against them Tertullian drew on a tradition going back to Zeno which stressed the continuity of substance between body and soul. The πνεῦμα is the warm breath that penetrates and animates all living things, clearly a material substance since it is related to air, fire (heat), and water (moisture). This is what leaves the body at death, and this is identified with soul. Zeno's theories were inspired by medical discoveries as well as philosophical sources, and Tertullian follows the Stoics in citing medical writers, expecially Soranus./4/

Tertullian offered the following evidence for the soul's corporeality in *De Anima* 5 and 6:

1) Zeno's argument that what causes the body to die by its leaving is corporeal. Spirit is what leaves. Therefore, the spirit is corporeal. Tertullian adds that this spirit is identical with the soul; therefore the soul is corporeal.
2) Cleanthes' observation that family likeness of psychic traits is passed on.
3) the "intercommunion of susceptibility" between body and soul in pain or emotion (ANF trans.).
4) the power of the soul to move the body.
5) the dependence of the soul on nourishment provided for the body.

Tertullian is open about his sources:

> I call on the Stoics also to help me, who, while declaring almost in our own terms that the soul is a spiritual essence (inasmuch as breath and spirit are in their nature very near akin to each other), will yet have no difficulty in persuading (us) that the soul is a corporeal substance./5/

Note that for Tertullian (as for the Stoics) there is no contradiction in affirming the corporeality of the soul and calling it a *spiritual* essence. This is why he could also assert that God was corporeal without any sense of violating the Scriptural claim that God is a spirit. Augustine is perfectly aware of the ambiguity of the terms *"corpus"* and *"spiritus"* (IV,36) and realizes that a statement like Tertullian's is operating with a different definition of *corpus* (IV,17). So although in the latter half of Book IV (chs. 17–35) Augustine points out to Victor the absurd consequences of holding that the soul's nature is corporeal, he nevertheless recognizes that their differences may be a quarrel over words, not substance./6/

Augustine also sees that Victor has misunderstood "incorporeal" as meaning either something airy or an empty void (III,18), an error which does not shock the author of the *Confessions*, who had struggled for years with his inability to imagine what a purely spiritual reality might be. /7/ Victor's insistence that the soul is a body (*corpus*) is a predictable mistake,/8/ as is his confusion over the distinction between *anima* and *spiritus* (IV,36–37), and Augustine is harder on the inconsistency and crudity of his arguments than on their premise.

In Epistle 166,4, to Jerome on the origin of the soul, Augustine discusses the problem of terminology:

> I do not wish to make a useless difficulty over terms, nor deserve to bring one down upon myself, since when there is a question of reality there is no need to quarrel over a word. Therefore, if the body is the whole substance or essence or whatever better term one can use to express what it is in itself, then the soul is a body. Likewise, if one chooses to call that alone incorporeal which is supremely unchangeable and everywhere wholly present, then the soul is a body, since of itself it is no such thing. Furthermore, if it is a characteristic of a body to occupy space with a certain length, width, and height, and for it to be so placed or moved that it fills a larger space with the larger part of itself, and a smaller space with a smaller part, and for the part to be less than the whole, then the soul is not a body. For, the soul extends through the whole body to which it imparts life, not by a distribution in space but by a certain life-giving impetus; it is wholly present in every smallest part, not less in smaller parts . . . but . . . wholly present in each and all parts. . . . Hence, it is clear that, whether the soul is to be called corporeal or incorporeal, it has a special nature created of a more excellent substance than all these elements of earthly material./9/

By this standard, it may seem strange that Augustine argues with Victor at all over the point. But a comparison of Epistle 190 from 418, three years after Epistle 166, shows a far less complaisant attitude toward the question of the soul's corporeality.

> Those who claim that souls are begotten from one which God gave to the first man . . . , if they follow the opinion of Tertullian, they certainly hold that such souls are not spirits but bodies, and are produced from corporeal seed—and what more perverted view could be expressed? . . . Any Christian who rejects this madness with heart and lips, and confesses that the soul is not body but spirit, as indeed it is . . . /10/

Coming across this *opusculum* at Peter's home, Victor could not have guessed that Augustine was willing to consider the argument a mere question of terminology.

But IV,17 and 18 show that Augustine's quarrel is more with Victor's inconsistency than with his definition:

> If a thing is not a body unless it consists of physical limbs, the earth will not be a body, nor sky, nor a stone, nor water, nor stars, nor anything of that sort. If, however, anything is a body which consists of larger or smaller parts taking up larger or smaller spaces, then all those things which I have just mentioned are bodies; air is a body, this visible light is a body, and so are all those things which the apostle calls "celestial bodies and terrestrial bodies." . . . You cause me some concern when you state; "If a soul lacks a body so as to be (as some would have it) an airy and futile substance of hollow emptiness. . . ." From these words of yours you seem to believe that everything which lacks body is devoid of substance. If that is the case, how do you dare to say that God lacks a body . . . ?

The term "airy substance" (*aeria substantia*) was ill-chosen too, for Augustine points out that air is a body and not mere emptiness: witness the resistance of the air in an inverted cup to the water in which it is immersed (IV,18). Victor has in fact missed the whole point of the Stoic observation that the soul *is* air, warm air, and that is why it is corporeal.

Victor relies more heavily than Tertullian on the association of visibility with corporeality. True, Tertullian used the example of Lazarus and Dives in which Victor followed suit, but his point was that the talk about bodily limbs indicated that the soul had the shape of the human body, not that the figures in the story could not have seen each other unless they were corporeal. In fact in Chapter 6 Tertullian gives examples to prove that corporeal organs perceive incorporeal things (e.g., the ear sound) and vice versa (e.g., the intellect the soul).

Tertullian does, however, grant visibility to the soul and reports the vision of a Montanist woman of his circle of a "soul in bodily shape . . . soft and transparent and of an ethereal colour . . ." (*De An.* 9). Victor is not so ingenuous as to repeat this story from a heretical sect as part of his proof, but he has on another point gone outside the canonical books for his examples. He offers Dinocrates, brother of the martyr Perpetua, as evidence that those who die unbaptized can be saved through intercession (I,12; II,16; III,12). Augustine disapproves of basing a dogmatic point on a noncanonical book (III,12), but since his opponent has brought up the dream, Augustine is quite ready to use it to refute Victor's notion of the soul as corporeal. Dinocrates appeared to Perpetua with his fatal wound on him. Why, asks Augustine, if he was indeed appearing to his sister in the sort of body Victor claims, had his soul not shown that remarkable ability to regenerate itself free from injury (IV,27)? Victor's attempts to relate the growth of soul to body follow Tertullian's to some extent: Tertullian finds it possible to speak of a "puberty of the soul" (*De An.* 38), and of length, breadth, and height (*De An.* 9), but denies that the soul can increase in substance (*De An.* 37). Rather its growth is "calling forth its powers."

The error of supposing the soul to be a sort of body is, for all the possible absurdities inherent in it, a "tolerable error in one who has not yet learned that there can be something which, though it is not a body, yet bears a certain likeness to a body" (I,5). Augustine finds it "tolerable" because he endured the same difficulty early in his career(*Conf.* V,19 and VII,1–2) and because he still thinks that the question is not central to the Catholic faith (II,4).

An early debate on this problem follows an almost identical line of argument to that of DNOA. In *De Quantitate Animae*, written in 387 or 388, Augustine starts from the premise that the soul does not have length, width, or solidity (ch. 4; cf. DNOA IV,17), to which Evodius objects (in the spirit of Victor) that "if the soul is none of these, it is practically nothing." Augustine then uses the example of "justice" as an entity which is real but not corporeal (ch.5 of *De Quant. An.*; cf. DNOA IV, 25 and CD VIII,5) as proof that it is not material, and in fact is superior to a material body (*De Quant. An.* 23; cf. DNOA IV,31). To Peter, Augustine remarks that the question is interesting but "I do not actually think there is any great harm to Christian teaching in not knowing about this. . . . One's conclusions are finally more complex than useful" (II,7).

As for the second part of Victor's objection, that soul and spirit are two distinct things, he can claim little support from Tertullian, who realizes just as well as Augustine the historical muddle that prevents an exact definition. The Stoic identification of πνεῦμα with soul, for all its claim that the soul was not complex but simple, yet recognized the possibility of speaking of "parts" of the soul. What those parts were and how many, the Stoic writers did not agree upon,/11/ but generally they included the five senses and some sort of division into rational and irrational elements. Augustine refers in IV,6 to the ἡγεμονικόν, a term used by Stoics and medical writers for the ruling element of the soul. Tertullian preferred to define these as *functions* of the soul rather than a division into parts (*De*

An. 13), and in chapter 18 says: "mind is nothing else than an apparatus or instrument of the soul, and . . . the spirit is no other faculty, separate from the soul, but is the soul itself exercised in respiration." His Stoic antecedents show up clearly in his connection of the spirit with respiration, even more clearly at *De Anima* 11: "We must call [the soul] spirit in a definitive sense—not because of its condition but of its action; not in respect of its nature, but of its operation; because it *respires*, and not because it is spirit in any special sense" (ANF trans.).

He remains true to the Stoic monism in his analysis of intellect and sense in chapter 18:

> For is it not true that to employ the senses is to use the
> intellect? And to employ the intellect amounts to a use of
> the senses (*intelligere sentire est*) ? What indeed can sen-
> sation be, but the understanding of that which is the object
> of the sensation? And what can the intellect or understand-
> ing be but the seeing of that which is the object under-
> stood? . . . If corporeal things are the objects of sense, and
> incorporeal ones objects of the intellect, it is the classes of
> the objects which are different, not the domicile or abode
> of sense and intellect; in other words not the soul (*anima*)
> and the mind (*animus*). (ANF trans.)

Tertullian is consistent in refusing to grant superiority to the intellect over the senses:

> How can a thing be superior to that which is instrumental
> to its existence, which is also indispensable to it, and to
> whose help it owes everything which it acquires? . . . The
> intellect is not to be preferred above the senses . . . and
> . . . the intellect must not be separated from the senses.
> (ch. 18, ANF)

Sensation comes from the soul, and opinion from sensation; and the whole (process) is the soul. (ch. 17, ANF) These passages are explicitly directed against Platonic dualism, which Tertullian regarded as the parent of Gnostic and docetist heresy.

One might expect Augustine, by contrast, to defend a Platonic tripartite division of man since he credits "the Platonists" with teaching him that there can be such a thing as an incorporeal, spiritual reality./12/ In the system of Plotinus the successive emanations from the One, the Noῦς, and the world-soul, are reflected in man's constitution of voῦς (mind or spirit) and ψυχή (soul, *anima*), the body being the third element. The πνεῦμα of Plotinus constitutes an intermediary between the descended soul and the body./13/ That trichotomy might appear to find Biblical confirmation in Paul's benediction (I Thess. 5:23): "May your spirit and soul and body be kept sound and blameless . . ." (RSV). However, in DNOA Augustine instead views *anima* as the inclusive name and *spiritus* as the soul's particular power of rational thought. He generally prefers to describe man as made up simply of body and soul./14/ Even where he uses the picture of a trinity in the human soul as an analogy of the divine Trinity, the division into memory, intelligence, and will does not name parts of the soul but rather the whole soul acting in a certain way. It may rather be *Victor*, given the eclecticism of the times, who has adopted Neoplatonic categories on this particular point.

Augustine, however, is not prepared to fight over it, merely to recognize it as a

> difficult problem, for divine Scripture speaks of "spirit" in many different ways and with various meanings—but what we are discussing now, that by which we reason and understand and acquire knowledge, we agree that this is properly called "spirit" and that this is not the whole soul but some [faculty] of it./15/

but he concludes that in a general sense soul and spirit may be used to designate the same incorporeal reality (IV,37). Again the problem grows out of a confusion in terminology rather than a disagreement in substance:

> Although it is agreed that there is something in the soul properly called "spirit," minus which it is still proper to speak of the soul, there is still no quarrel over the thing itself, since plainly I say the same as you do: that what is properly called "spirit" is that by which we reason and understand when the [faculties] are distinguished. . . . (IV,36)

What Augustine really dislikes is Victor's rather simple-minded extension of Tertullian's transparent *Doppelgänger* to a third figure, the spirit (IV,20).

Why does Augustine choose to define man as body and soul rather than adopting the three-fold division? The decisive reason is Biblical language.

> À mesure qu'il progresse dans ses recherches, l'influence platonicienne est de plus en plus contrebalancée par l'influ-

ence biblique qui, acceptée dès le début comme décisive
en droit, devient en fait dominante, non seulement dans sa
pensée, mais dans son vocabulaire./16/

G. Verbeke comes to the same conclusion in asking the more general question of why Christians held on to πνεῦμα at all as their
term for a spiritual reality when it had been so heavily associated
with materialist philosophy. His answer is: because of the Old Testament;/17/ the Genesis account wherein man, formed from clay
and breathed upon by God, became "a living soul"/18/ determined
the Christian conception of man.

Verbeke also sees the Book of Wisdom (from the first century
B.C.) as an important influence on the Christian Fathers./19/ Its
author, an Alexandrian Jew acquainted with Stoicism, uses πνεῦμα
and ψυχή as synonyms; but unlike the Stoics, he makes the human
soul a work of God, not a particle of His being. The Holy Spirit,
Wisdom herself, is also πνεῦμα, but she is the breath of God which
permeates all beings ("The Spirit of the Lord fills the world," Wisd.
1:7, RSV) and the representation of divine activity in the world.

This double meaning of "πνεῦμα" and the ambiguity of "*anima*"
necessitated a constant vigilance within the Church vis-à-vis the
tendency to identify the soul with God—to make, in fact, the mistake which Augustine lists first among Victor's serious errors.

Having disposed of Victor's criticisms as quarrels over words,
Augustine moves on to set his own agenda for debate by citing
eleven errors that to him are matters of substance, not words only.
One can divide them into theoretical (1–5) and practical (6–11)
questions and more specifically into three categories:

1) the relationship of the soul to God (1–2).
2) the relationship of sin to the soul (3–5).
3) the necessity of baptism (6–11).

Against these Augustine places three requirements which hold no
matter what theory of the soul's origin one chooses:

1) the soul must be distinguished from God.
2) the soul brings with it to birth no merits or demerits.
3) baptism is necessary for salvation.

The Introduction pointed out that Augustine's purpose in writing was pragmatic, not merely theoretical, and the fact that the last
six errors deal with baptism—a matter of great consequence for
church life and order—illustrates this practical intent of the trea-

tise. The connection of baptism with the controversy over the soul's origin, perhaps not an obvious one, will be explained at the appropriate point, after the fifth error. But first the errors in order.

The first error: "Noli credere, noli dicere, noli docere quod non de nihilo, sed de sua natura fecerit animam Deus, si vis esse catholicus." (I,4; I,24; II,4–6; III,3; III,7)

The Christian insistence on the created status of the soul and consequent distinction from God is perhaps the place where Christian theology runs most irreconcilably head-on into an opposing Greek belief. Christian orthodoxy maintained that the soul was a product of creation, not an emanation from, or a particle of, the Creator. Greek philosophy was convinced of the continuity between God and the human soul. By calling the soul immortal (for which he won the approval of the Christian Fathers), Plato bestowed on it the most distinctive characteristic of divinity, for the gods of Greek religion were οἱ ἀθάνατοι, the ones who cannot die, the immortals. Plotinus viewed human souls as emanations from the One and hence as only uneasily reconciled to union with the body and as hungry for return to the "homeland."/20/

Stoicism believed in cosmic unity, the harmony of all elements of the universe: the divine Logos penetrates all, and human logos, the reasoning power of the soul, manifests its presence. Even Epicureanism, mistrusted as atheism among both pagan and Christian writers, included gods and souls alike in the flux of the atoms.

Christians were quite ready to make use of classical ideas on the soul where they suited a particular apologetic purpose, e.g., immortality of the soul. However, the Genesis creation account compelled them to admit a break in the assumed continuity between God and soul and to substitute similarity of another sort, the *imago Dei*. Since God made man "in his image," Christians could agree with the Greek conviction that the universe and its laws were intelligible to man. Nevertheless, they insisted that whatever similarity existed between God and man was the result of God's creative action, not an accidental or inevitable natural phenomenon nor a proof that man and God shared a common nature.

The Church was challenged perennially to defend its position against various gnostic heresies which viewed souls as divine emanations entrapped temporarily in corrupt bodies: The Manichaean and Priscillianist heresies are examples from Augustine's time, and Augustine fears Victor's contamination by the latter (III,9).

The quotations from Victor at I,4; II,5; and III,3 /21/ show that he wished to avoid these errors, but his rejection of creation from nothing or from another created substance left him with no alternative, and in II,5 Augustine accuses him of using the word "emanated." If Victor rejects the two former choices and supports the latter, he abolishes the distinction between Creator and creature, supposes that the immutable God produces from Himself a mutable nature, and identifies God with the raw material of His own creation—all unacceptable consequences. Moreover it would end in the blasphemous assertion that, in the case of the wicked, God condemns a part of Himself to eternal punishment (II,6).

Tertullian too had spoken of the soul as "sprung from the breath of God"/22/ but had made a careful distinction between breath of God and God's spirit in the sense of Holy Spirit./23/

> We, however, who allow no appendage to God (in the sense
> of equality), by this very fact reckon the soul as very far
> below God: for we suppose it to be born, and hereby to
> possess something of a diluted divinity and an attenuated
> felicity, as the breath (of God), though not His Spirit. . . .
> Although immortal . . . [the soul is] yet . . . passible . . .
> and consequently from the first capable of deviation from
> perfection and right. (*De An.* 24, ANF)

Even more specifically in *Adversus Marcionem* II,9, Tertullian shows the difference between God's nature and His breath, which animates man. The spirit which God breathes into man is the *image* of His own spirit, and will thus

> be less than the reality. . . . While it possesses beyond
> doubt the true lineaments of divinity, such as an immortal
> soul, freedom and its own mastery over itself, foreknowl-
> edge in a great degree, reasonableness, capacity of under-
> standing and knowledge, it is even in these respects an im-
> age still, and never amounts to the actual power of Deity,
> nor to absolute exemption from fault. (ANF trans.)

If Victor had read this treatise (and some of his examples make it seem probable that he had), still he did not make use of it for ammunition.

There are other examples of Victor's using illustrations or wordings that seem to come from Tertullian, but these are applied to other points or are used to draw different conclusions. Tertullian uses the simile of a man blowing into a flute (*Adv. Marc.* II,9), which does not thereby become human, to illustrate that though man is a living soul, he has not a life-giving spirit. Victor uses the simile of a man blowing up a balloon (*uter*) to show that one can breathe out of one's own substance and yet remain undiminished (III,4). Augustine is quick to point out the faulty reasoning here: that the breath with which one inflates a balloon is merely from the surrounding air, not from one's own substance. While he is at it, he has a good time puncturing Victor's inflated ego (III,5). Victor also points to Elisha's raising of the widow's son as a sign that God could be undiminished in substance while giving man a soul (cf. *Adv. Marc.* II,9). This Augustine finds an even more inappropriate analogy, for Victor has seemed to imply that human breath *can* be life-giving, whereas Tertullian makes the point that it is not.

Whether Victor was as careful as Tertullian to separate the soul from its creator, or original from image, is impossible to tell from Augustine's quotations. Moreover, it is a commonplace of debate to overstate one's opponent's arguments./24/ But Victor has made his position less defensible by adopting part of Tertullian's solution and rejecting part. What his predecessor claimed only for the soul of Adam, Victor attempts to claim for every soul. Tertullian is able to stand on solid Scriptural evidence for Adam's ensoulment by the breath of God; but as a traducianist, he does not need to make any such claims for the souls of any subsequent human beings, including Eve. Victor tries to extend Tertullian's explanation of Adam's ensoulment to all his descendants and fails to find any Scriptural evidence that could not as well be used to support traducianism (I,17–20). Perhaps Victor's purpose in saying God is incorporeal was to make it clear that the corporeal soul could not be of the same substance as God. But the departure from Tertullian here only runs him into another difficulty, viz., that of seeming to say that God is unreal.

The second error: "Noli credere . . . per infinitum tempus atque ita semper Deum animas dare, sicut semper est ipse qui dat." (III,8)

Augustine's objection to Victor's sentence appears to be a case of misplaced emphasis. The Bishop takes his opponent to mean that God will continue to give souls through all eternity just as He exists for all eternity. That is a legitimate inference from the Latin, but the sentence can also be taken in a more orthodox sense: that it is

God, the God who was and is and will be, who alone gives souls. Victor's formulation is interesting because it offers strong support for a connection between the circle of Optatus (to whom are addressed letters 190 and 202A) and Victor's audience. Epistle 202A, 7–8, informs us that Optatus had been caught in the middle of a controversy between traducianists and creationists within his bishopric. His letter to Augustine, to which 202A was the reply, was not so much an inquiry about Augustine's own opinion as a plea for Augustine's backing against the traducianists. In chapter 9 of the letter, there is a reference to a panel of secular judges called in to arbitrate the question. De Veer says, "One would not be surprised to discover—but how?—that Vincent Victor was among them; the point of view which he will later defend, with a certain peevishness against Augustine as though he had been personally offended by him, is that of Optatus and the judges."/25/

This error of Victor's calls to mind a recurring idea in Epistle 202A which Augustine quotes from Optatus' letter. It appears in two forms:

1) . . . Deum fecisse homines et facere et facturum esse, neque aliquid esse in caelis aut in terra quod non ipso constiterit et constet auctore. (chs. 8 and 13)

2) Deus auctor universarum rerum hominumque cunctorum et fuit et est et futurus est. (chs. 11, 12, and 13)

The emphasis on past, present, and future is for Optatus' party clearly an important part of their creationist stand. Further, in Epistle 190,1, Augustine, apparently quoting or paraphrasing Optatus' position, alludes to John 5:17 ("Pater meus usque modo operatur"):

. . . whether the all-powerful Creator, who undoubtedly "worketh until now" creates new souls for individual persons without any root-stock. (FOC trans.)

The affirmation of God's continuing creative action in past, present, and future appears to have been a catchword for the creationists, and Victor's emphasis on time (per infinitum tempus . . . semper . . . semper) looks like his variation on that same theme.

Victor may mean only that it is *God* who gives souls. Epistle 202A indicates that Optatus understood his adversaries as denying that the soul came from God by attributing it to propagation. That may be a case of Optatus misrepresenting or at least misunderstanding *his* opponents. Whether the charge was true or not, the creationists wished to emphasize both the continuity of God's activity and His identity as sole creator. The clause "sicut semper est ipse qui dat" probably meant to Victor that God is the one who always gives; to Augustine it meant that God continues to give souls forever, just as He exists forever. That smacks of some sort of eternal return theory, and Augustine will not let it go unchallenged. The Latin is ambiguous. To someone searching for possible errors it invites misinterpretation. But Optatus' formula—*fecisse, facere, facturum* or *fuisse, esse, futurum*—arouses no criticism from Augustine in Epistle 202A. I believe it is safe to say that Victor only intended to represent Optatus' thoroughly orthodox view. (See p. 64 below)

The third error: "Noli credere . . . animam meritum aliquod perdidisse per carnem, tamquam boni meriti fuerit ante carnem." (I,6; II,18; III,9; IV,16)

Victor has gotten himself into deep water here, for his assumptions seem to be

1) that the soul existed somewhere before its incarnation in flesh,
2) that it had some power of good or evil action in its preexistent state, and
3) that incarnation is a bad thing (a conclusion Augustine draws from Victor's words in I,6).

Augustine is not altogether hostile to the idea that souls might preexist their entry into flesh. In Epistle 166,7, Augustine names for Jerome four opinions on the origin of the soul which he had put forward some 20 years earlier (around 395) in *De Libero Arbitrio* (III,57–59); two of these opinions suppose the soul's preexistence. In *De Genesi ad Litteram* VII and X (the two books which deal specifically with the nature and origin of the soul), Augustine examines the relationship of Adam's soul and subsequent individual souls to that creative act of God recounted in Genesis 1:27. His conclusions, though they are tentatively held, include the following:

1) that man is among the creations of the six-day period of Genesis 1–2, but that the man Adam is not (Gen 1:27 and 2:7),
2) that *creatio ex nihilo* does not take place after the six-day period of Genesis 1–2 (Gen. 2:1–2).

These conclusions entail, if not an actual preexistence, at least a logical or ideal one, where the soul created by God is the prototype of all subsequent souls./26/

Besides the Genesis passages cited above, Sirach 18:1—"He created all things at one time" (*creavit omnia simul*)—keeps reappearing as the exegetical principle by which the Genesis accounts are interpreted, implying that all souls, as well as other things, originate from that primal creative act of God.

For Plato, preexistence solved both an epistemological and a moral difficulty. Plato's theory of recollection (*Phaedo, Meno*) said that the soul contemplated the Forms in a previous existence so that learning—of mathematical truths, for example—is a process of remembering. Augustine's description of learning as remembering, particularly in *De Magistro*, and his understanding of the powers of *memoria* (*Conf.*X,17–19) seem at first to rest on the same assumption: the preexistence of the soul. The young Augustine may actually have held the Platonic view,/27/ though he denies it in the *Retractations* (I,8,2). Plato's version of the transmigration of souls in *Republic* X (614b–621d, the Myth of Er) accounted for the apparently undeserved innate differences which we see in moral character among humans and justly assigned rewards and punishments.

In Plotinus, the World-Soul is a divine emanation from the *Nous* (Mind, the world of the intelligible Forms), which emanates in turn from the One. Particular souls descend from the World-Soul, by a natural process, into the world of matter, the last, and so least real, product of emanation. The same ambivalence so prominent in Christian writers toward the physical world is found already in Plotinus./28/ Of itself the material world is not evil, but man easily falls into the sin of pride (τόλμα), Augustine's *superbia*) or becomes too preoccupied with the ordering of what is beneath him and forgets that the soul is the true self. The individual soul may pass through a series of bodies in its progress toward reunification with the One.

Among Augustine's Christian predecessors, Origen had tried to solve the moral difficulty of undeserved suffering and "to establish the impartiality and justice of God" by Platonic means./29/ Souls "fell" into union with flesh as a result of sins committed in a heavenly realm. Earthly existence was thus a punishment, the outcome of mistaken use of free will rather than fulfillment of a divine purpose.

The Church had condemned these teachings so recently (400)

that Augustine thinks Victor may not know that he is proposing heresy (III,9). The Priscillianist sect, mentioned in the same passage, was one of those which preserved Origenist ideas and survived by at least 200 years its official censure in 380.

Preexistence of the soul Augustine might have tolerated, but the implication that its embodiment was an evil was now declared unorthodox. Augustine himself

> did change his conception of man's primitive state. Previously he had taken the view that man was created with an ethereal body and was not subject to death and had no sexuality until after his sin, when the body became gross, earthy, more like the animals. But in the sixth book of the Genesis Commentary (VI, 19:30 through 29:40) he reversed his position. /30/

It seems to us obvious that the Biblical account includes the whole human being—body and soul, male and female—in God's judgment that all was "very good." But the strong Platonic bias in favor of the soul as superior, as the true self, and its distrust of what was corporeal colored the Christian reading of Genesis for a long time. /31/

The preexistence problem figures in Augustine's criticism of Victor; so does the matter of baptism. Victor thinks he has found a way to avoid making God responsible for original sin by attributing it to the soul's union with flesh./32/ But he says Augustine will object on the grounds that it would be inappropriate for the soul to be sanctified in baptism by way of the flesh when it was through flesh that it was defiled (II,11). Then he adds ironically that perhaps Augustine thinks baptism only cleanses the body and not the soul or spirit. Augustine ignores the gibe but protests that Victor is assuming a preexistent soul while claiming not to:

> How can he claim in another passage that he has "always maintained that the soul is not from propagation nor from nothing nor existent by its own powers nor preexistent to the body"? (II,11)

The inconsistency becomes more glaring with

The fourth error: "Noli credere . . . animam per carnem reparare habitudinem priscam et per illam renasci, per quam meruerat inquinari." (I,6; II,11; III,10)

The beginning is again a reference to baptism. *Per illam* and

per quam are references to *carnem*, i.e., the flesh is what receives
baptism and the flesh is that by which the soul was deservedly defiled. The contradiction is clear. *Habitudo prisca* implies a former
state of goodness or innocence; *meruerat inquinari* implies one of
evil or guilt. Even if the doctrine of preexistence were true, Victor's
logic would be faulty. And a preexistence with good or evil actions
attached to it is against Scripture's statement that those not yet born
have done neither good nor evil./33/

The fifth error: "Noli credere . . . quod anima meruerit esse peccatrix ante omne peccatum." (I,8–9; 33–34; II,12–14; III,11)

Augustine adds to this quotation another, which apparently followed on it:

> Anima itaque si peccatrix esse meruit, quae peccatrix esse
> non potuit, neque in peccato remansit, quia in Christo
> praefigurata in peccato esse non debuit, sicut esse non po-
> tuit./34/ (III,11)

DeVeer /35/ notices a parallel with Tertullian's *Adversus Marcionem*
II,9,8, where *adflatus* refers to the breath that constitutes the soul:
"hoc ipsum ergo potuit adflatus Dei admittere, potuit, sed non debuit." With this distinction Tertullian loosens the knot of God's responsibility for sin: the soul is capable of sin because its breath is
only the image of God's spirit, not the substance. Nevertheless it
ought to have refrained from sin because it was warned, "which was
meant to be a support for its slender nature, and a direction for its
liberty of choice" (ANF). Sin is attributed to the soul's own free will,
not to its affinity with God. There is no hint of this choice's belonging to some previous existence, but since the text is only about
Adam, that question does not arise.

Victor's passage may be an imitation of Tertullian. If so, it is odd
that he does not take advantage of his arguments. One suspects that
his deliberately paradoxical statement aims more at rhetorical effect
than elucidation. There is a parallel placement of infinitives, of
forms of *peccatum*, and of the final rhyming verbs. The two beginning clauses and the two endings are set up symmetrically:

peccatrix esse meruit	esse non debuit
peccatrix esse non potuit	esse non potuit.

This is perhaps an instance of what Augustine was thinking of when
he concluded his book (IV,39) with the observation that

> the striking effect and tempo of your recitation . . . the
> wealth of words and the versatility and natural quality of
> your genius. . . .

probably overwhelmed Victor's listeners and dulled their critical
faculties so that they did not pay proper attention to the arguments
themselves.

Augustine ignores the phrase "prefigured in Christ" in the foregoing quotation, though it might have been an important part of the
argument. There are no other clues to what Victor meant by it.
DeVeer suggests a possible interpretation:

> Arguait-il d'une relation de l'âme au Christ, dans sa créa-
> tion et sa rédemption, autre, plus générale et plus efficace
> que celle constituée par le baptême, relation que seul le
> péché personnel de l'homme adulte pourrait briser? Je son-
> gerais volontiers à l'image de Dieu en nous, et qui est le
> reflet de l'image du Christ, mais ce n'est qu'une hypothèse
> . . . qui d'ailleurs nous conduirait encore vers l'origén-
> isme./36/

Again Augustine sees in this statement of Victor's the Origenist assumption that the soul's embodiment was a punishment for some
previous sin. How else can one interpret his use of the word *meruit*? Augustine thinks Victor's *non potuit* must mean that the soul
was unable to sin before it was joined to flesh; if that is so, this
clause, coupled with *meruit* is nonsense./37/

The last six errors all have to do with infant baptism, which
might, at first glance, seem unrelated to the problem of the soul's
origin. Their inclusion, however, demonstrates the practical consequences of holding one theory or the other and reveals that this
debate is for Augustine not simply an academic exercise./38/ A creationist like Victor who believes that the soul comes directly from
God's inbreathing will be hard-pressed to account for the presence
of sin in the soul of a newborn child. He will, in Augustine's opinion, either be tempted to say that the soul of an infant is without
sin at birth and hence that baptism is not an urgent necessity (the
solution the Pelagians favored) or to attribute to a good God the
creation of a corrupted nature.

A useful document for understanding the connection between
creationism and baptism is Augustine's letter 166 to Jerome. It is all
the more instructive as a comparison with DNOA because it is written in 415, early on in the Pelagian controversy, and because it
shows a more sympathetic side to Augustine's nature than some of

his later pronouncements on the fate of children. Augustine lays out all his premises and confesses his difficulty with creationism very candidly. The letter, or rather book, as Augustine refers to it later, /39/ accepts as incontrovertible fact the universality of human sin even in newborn children. The Biblical proofs for holding this belief are particularly Rom. 5:12–19, I Cor. 15:22–23, and Job 14:4–5 (LXX)./40/

Augustine's second line of proof, that from Church tradition, seems to a modern reader somewhat forced; we might be inclined to read the Church's practice of baptizing infants as a sign that remission of sins is a gift. Augustine takes it as a proof that infants must be sinful since otherwise there would be no point to baptizing them *in remissionem peccatorum*./41/ Peter Brown calls this "Augustine's trump card" against Julian of Eclanum and a point where Augustine departs from rational argument to "appeal to dangerously primitive layers of feeling" about long-standing tradition, amounting to plain superstition among the Bishop's congregation./42/ The priest Peter comes in for that kind of heavy reminder in II,15–17, where Victor's pronouncements on baptism attract the damning adjectives "novel," "foreign to the Church's discipline," and "opposed to the firmly-established Catholic faith."

On the other side is the unshakeable conviction that "God is good, God is just, God is almighty" (Epistle 166,16). Augustine inclines toward creationism rather than traducianism (ch. 27), but given the above requirements—the innate sinfulness of man and the goodness of God—Augustine is stuck at an agonizing impasse:

> Tell me, if souls are individually created today for individuals at birth, *when* these souls commit sin in infants so as to need remission of sin in the sacrament of Christ . . . ; or if they do not sin, how can it be just of the Creator to bind them to another's sin when they are joined to mortal bodies descended from [Adam], so that damnation is their lot unless help is given them by the Church, yet it is not in their power to be helped by the grace of baptism? (ch. 10, FOC trans.)

This letter, 166, contains a good deal of what, only four years later, Augustine will scornfully dismiss as an unallowable *misericordia*, /43/ i.e., a tormenting anguish over the fate of children—not just the theoretical question of their eternal fate but their present totally undeserved sufferings (ch. 16).

His later hardening of attitude into what seems a heartless dis-

regard for simple human kindness parallels the increasing danger
he perceives in Pelagian teachings. In order to defend what he considers the irrefutable evidence of Scripture that in Adam all have
sinned and thereby to uphold the grace of God, he must finally
maintain that unbaptized infants are condemned. In a letter to Pau-
linus of Nola, /44/ Romans 9:15 and Exodus 33:19 are interpreted
thus:

> What did he here teach us but that, as death is the just due
> of the clay of the first man, it belongs to the mercy of God
> and not to the merits of man that *anyone* is saved, and that
> therein there is no injustice with God, because He is not
> unjust either in forgiving or in exacting the penalty. Mercy
> is free where just vengeance could be taken. (FOC transl.
> Italics mine.)/45/

God is, in the parallelism of DNOA IV,16, both *misericordissimus
gratiae largitor* and at the same time *iustissimus supplicii retribu-
tor*.

His very last writings aroused the civilized fury of Julian of
Eclanum:

> "Tiny babies," you say, "are not weighed down by their own
> sin but are burdened with the sin of another." Tell me then
> . . . tell me: who is this person who inflicts punishment on
> innocent creatures . . . ? You answer: God. God, you say!
> God! He Who "commended His love to us," Who "has loved
> us," Who "has not spared His own Son for us. . . ." He it is,
> you say, Who judges in this way; He is the persecutor of
> newborn children; He it is who sends tiny babies to eternal
> flames. . . . It would be right and proper to treat you as
> beneath argument: you have come so far from religious feel-
> ing, from civilized thinking, so far, indeed, from mere com-
> mon sense, in that you think that your Lord God is capable
> of committing a crime against justice such as is hardly con-
> ceivable even among the barbarians./46/

Julian hits a weak point in Augustine's position, for it is certainly
difficult to reconcile it with what the New Testament tells of God's
love and His will for the salvation of all people./47/

Victor's last six errors all have to do with baptism and all reflect
a desire to avoid condemning the unbaptized. None of them, however, is based on a denial of original sin, as Augustine observes
(III,19). Victor has developed his own peculiar connection between
creationism and baptism in order to reconcile his theories of the
soul with original sin. In I,6 and II,13 he is quoted as saying that

although God suffers the soul to be defiled by its union with flesh, He provides a way for it also to be purified by the flesh, viz., baptism. Augustine protests that then baptism becomes merely God's way of correcting a botched job of creation (II, 13):

> If He frees from sin those innocent and pure souls which He Himself involved in sin, He heals a wound which He inflicted on us, not one which He found in us. God forbid . . . ! (I, 7)

Augustine cannot accuse Victor of Pelagianism but he does warn him that his views on baptism are likely to lead him toward the recently-condemned heresy, indicating that he does not think it is Pelagius who has led Victor astray. The errors could reasonably be attributed to Origenist or Priscillianist influence (III, 9) since Augustine names Origen among the *misericordes* whom he condemns in *City of God* XXI, 17. /48/

The sixth error: "Noli credere . . . infantes antequam baptizentur morte praeventos pervenire posse ad originalium indulgentiam peccatorum." (I, 33; II, 14; III, 12; IV, 16)

Unfortunately we cannot see *how* Victor has in mind to deliver the unbaptized from original sin apart from baptism; we see only that God's foreknowledge and mercy are involved (III, 19). Perhaps also the "prefigured in Christ" remark (I, 8), if we had more of the context, might have offered a clue. Victor does, however, provide us with two examples which purport to show the admission of the unbaptized to a blessed state after death: the repentant thief and Dinocrates, brother of the martyr Perpetua.

In I, 11 Augustine is willing to regard the thief as a special case because of his baptism by blood. /49/ Augustine lyrically describes his faith and hope which are accounted to him as a type of baptism. But he then makes the rather pedestrian suggestion that the water from Jesus' side might have sprinkled the thief or that he might already have been baptized. In his earlier works /50/ Augustine regarded the thief as an unbaptized man. His change of opinion is surely due to Pelagian opposition. His argument that the thief might even have been baptized in prison is somewhat anachronistic, not to mention that a baptized thief rather spoils the point of Luke's story. Augustine is right in challenging Victor's argument from silence, but his own argument is far-fetched.

The same criticism holds for the story of Dinocrates. Augustine brings up Dinocrates' age, seven years, to show that he is no longer *infans* and therefore is disqualified from proving the forgiveness of *original* sin. If he is old enough to have answered the questions in the baptismal rite for himself (and Augustine again points out that we do not know whether he might not have been baptized), he is also old enought to have committed sins for which he is responsible. Anyway, says Augustine, one ought not to base a doctrinal point on a noncanonical book. Having said this, however, Augustine demonstrates his complete willingness to use a noncanonical book for purposes of illustration when dogma is not at stake. The extraordinary accounts of Perpetua's dreams make admirable material for Augustine's exposition of the absurdities Victor has fallen into in his description of the soul's properties (IV,26–27).

In attacking this error, Augustine shows already an intransigence fortified by the Pelagians. At I,34 he says of creationists,

> Let them not say that little ones who die without baptism are able to obtain eternal life or the kingdom of heaven, absolved of their original sin by some other means [than baptism],

thus closing a loophole which Victor might have sought to leave open in his statement reported at III,19:

> If by chance anyone should object to the temporary assignment of the souls of the thief or of Dinocrates to paradise— for the prize of the kingdom of heaven still waits for them in the resurrection, although that principal [Dominical] saying counts against it, viz., "unless one is born again of water and the Spirit, he cannot enter into the kingdom"— nevertheless let him have my ungrudging assent if only he magnifies both the result and the working out (*et effectum et affectum*) of the divine mercy and foreknowledge.

Although Augustine had by this time suppressed the "desire to dilute this fact" (IV,16), scholasticism later managed to find a solution that both recognized the fact of original sin and "magnified the divine mercy" by distinguishing between a natural and supernatural order. The former carried with it a natural state of blessedness belonging to all human beings, including infants who die without baptism. The supernatural was the state of special grace and spiritual life given by God over and above anything that a creature could achieve unassisted./51/ Augustine's insight that evil was not the positive force the Manichaeans made it but rather the deprivation of good/52/ contributed to the solution. Human nature as God created it was whole, its fallen nature, wounded by sin, showed a privation of the original state of grace. If original sin was privative, then so must its punishment be. Infants would suffer the pain of loss and the deprivation of the beatific vision, but not the pain of sense. The development in the Middle Ages of the concept of a limbo for unbaptized infants included the notion of a restoration of the fullness of human nature.

The seventh error: "Noli credere . . . quos Dominus praedestinavit ad baptismum, praedestinationi eius eripi posse et ante defungi quam in eis fuerit quod Omnipotens praedestinavit inpletum." (II,13; III,13)

Victor has entangled himself in another logical difficulty here. How can it make sense to speak of God's predestination of something that is never in fact going to happen? If He predestines a child for baptism and death intervenes, then "fortune or fate or some other thing" (II,13) is granted a power greater than God's. Or else God is shown not to have known that the child would die and thus His foreknowledge is denied./53/ Some writers of the time had apparently used the argument of God's foreknowledge to assign rewards and punishments to children who die, on the grounds that God knew what sort of life they *would* have lived had they survived childhood (I,15). Augustine refutes their opinion at some length (although he admits Victor's innocence of this heresy [I,14]), as though this were a common way of justifying God's act in condemning unbaptized infants. His objection to them is the same as to Error Seven: how can God foreknow what never happens?

Probably Augustine is pressing the word *praedestinavit* beyond the sense that Victor intended for it./54/ The latter may mean only in a general sense that the child was "predestined to baptism" because its parents had the intention of bringing it to the sacrament and then were frustrated in their desire. In Augustine's treatment of the repentant thief and Cyprian's earlier handling,/55/ one can see the beginnings of what was later enunciated as the "baptism of desire" and the "baptism of blood." Victor would perhaps have wished to make this a case of the former.

The eighth error: "Noli credere . . . de infantibus qui, priusquam renascantur in Christo, praeveniuntur occiduo, scriptum esse: 'Raptus est, ne malitia mutet illius intellectum aut ne fictio decipiat animam eius. Propter hoc properavit de medio iniquitatis illum educere; placita enim erat Deo anima eius,' et: 'Consummatus in brevi replevit tempora longa.'" (II,13; III,14) (In Book II the seventh and eighth errors are treated as one.)

Victor is close to denying original sin here, implying that the child is snatched away by death lest some primal innocence be lost. Augustine recognizes it as a serious attack on baptism, for it leaves the unbaptized child in better shape than the one who waits around long enough to be baptized. He is content to rebuke Victor in strong terms (III,14), but he turns the full force of his irony on Peter (II,13):

> Who would refuse to have this man as his teacher? Would [he have us believe that] . . . if these [infants] were to linger just long enough in this life to die right after baptism, "wickedness perverts their understanding and falsehood deceives their souls"? And that to avoid this contingency it is to their advantage to be snatched away before they are baptized? And that in the very act of baptism they are changed for the worse and deceived by falsehood if it is *after* baptism that they are snatched away? O admirable doctrine, worthy of adherence!

The ninth error: "Noli credere . . . aliquas mansionum esse extra regnum Dei, quas esse Dominus dixit in domo Patris sui." (II,14; III,15–17)

The relevant texts are:

1) John 14:2: "In my Father's house are many mansions."
2) John 3:5: "Unless one is born again of water and the Spirit, he cannot enter the kingdom of God."

Victor, Augustine, and Pelagius each present a different version of the fate of the unbaptized, but their differences only prove that it is impossible to live with just two choices—heaven and hell. Augustine does his best, and when cornered by the Pelagians, asserts that there is no middle ground, *quasi medium locum* (I,11), between damnation and the kingdom of heaven. But in his first treatise against them, *De Peccatorum Meretis et Remissione, et de Baptismo Parvulorum,* Augustine allowed that the condemnation of children must be the "mildest of all," (I,21) and even in *Contra Julianum* (V,44) of 421 he admitted that since infants' punishment is only for original sin, not personal, it would be light. (Julian had said that by Augustine's reckoning it would be better for children never to have existed at all.) While denying the middle ground, he is compelled to admit there must be degrees in rewards and punishments. He makes John 3:5 absolute and refuses to grant any of the "mansions" to the unbaptized.

Pelagius also takes John 3:5 in a strict sense and excludes the unbaptized from the kingdom of God. But since infants have no sin when they enter the world, baptism "for the remission of sins" is unnecessary for them, nor do they merit any sort of punishment. God's gifts of salvation and eternal life are theirs by nature, even without baptism, though they are denied the special grace of entering the kingdom.

Victor, with his characteristic literalness, wishes to distinguish God's house from the kingdom of God. III,16 is written entirely in indirect discourse but not reproducing a point of Victor's. III,17, "*hoc qui dicunt*," indicates that Augustine is assuming that his correspondent's arguments, if fully given, would resemble those that Augustine has encountered elsewhere. He grants that if the "kingdom of God" is to mean every realm under God's power, even hell itself will be included (III,17); but he points out that this surely cannot be the meaning of John 3:5 nor of the petition "Thy kingdom come." It is not clear from III,15–19 just what distinction Victor wishes to make between the kingdom of God and the kingdom of heaven. If the mansions outside the kingdom of God (III,15) are identified with the "paradise" of the eleventh error, then it appears that Victor is using "kingdom of God" and "kingdom of heaven" as synonyms. But Augustine assumes that he is not at II,16, though in the next chapter he says that the question is immaterial. He does object, however, to separating parts of God's house from His kingdom, as though God had less power than an earthly king to rule over what belongs to Him (III,15). He has offered a similar objection to Pelagius/56/ for attempting to separate eternal life and salvation from the kingdom of God. All these are conferred by baptism and cannot be conferred without baptism. In fact Augustine even seems to extend that condition to include the sacrament of the Eucharist also, for he uses John 6:53 as a proof text./57/

The development of the doctrine of limbo recognized points on both sides of the debate. The description in the 1907 edition of the *Catholic Encyclopedia* (to use a fairly recent, but pre-Vatican-II, example) of the fate of unbaptized infants clearly draws on both Augustinian and Pelagian elements:

> The Catholic teaching is uncompromising on this point, that all who depart this life without baptism, be it of water, or blood, or desire, are perpetually excluded from the vision of God. . . . As to the exact state of these souls in the next world [Catholic theologians] are not agreed. . . . Unbaptized infants are not unjustly deprived of heaven. The vision of God is not something to which human beings have a natural claim. . . . No injustice is involved when an undue privilege is not conferred upon a person. Original sin deprived the human race of an unearned right to heaven. Through the divine mercy this bar to the enjoyment of God is removed by baptism; but if baptism be not conferred, original sin remains, and the unregenerated soul, having no claim on heaven, is not unjustly excluded from it./58/

Even this looks rigid by the standards of post-Vatican-II theology, which has stressed the efficacy of the redemptive activity of Christ rather than its restrictions. Augustine's concern in refusing to let go of baptism as the only cure for sin was not a preoccupation with ecclesiastical authority but with what he perceived as the *sine qua non* of the Christian faith—human need of, and God's provision for, redemption. At its root, the Pelagian system had no need for Christ. He was useful by his example as Adam was harmful by his, but "grace" in Pelagius' writings meant only the natural endowments which man enjoyed by virtue of creation in God's image. Augustine saw the denial of the necessity for baptism as a denial of the necessity for redemption. Thonnard speculates:

> Si Vincent Victor ou Pélage avaient présenté ainsi leur doctrine, en maintenant la peine du dam et surtout en insistant, comme font les théologiens modernes, sur le rôle du Christ Rédempteur dans le sort de ces petits non baptisés, saint Augustin n'y aurait rien objecté, car c'est précisément ce qu'il demandait à saint Jérôme et à Optat comme au prêtre Pierre et à Vincent Victor à propos de l'origine des âmes par créatianisme./59/

The tenth error: "Noli credere . . . sacrificium Christianorum pro eis qui non baptizati de corpore exierint offerendum." (I,10; I,13; II,14; II,21; III,18)

Augustine gives Victor credit for wishing to compensate for his depreciation of baptism (I,10) by substituting some other sacramen-

tal grace. But counting against Victor's suggestion are its novelty
(II,15) and its dissimilarity with the Old Testament analogy Victor
draws. /60/ Augustine is also plainly riled by Victor's arrogant tone
in saying "It is my judgment that . . ." (*censeo*):

> non ait "puto," non ait "existimo," non ait "arbitror," non ait
> saltem "suggero" vel "dico" sed "censeo," ut scilicet, si of-
> fenderemur novitate seu perversitate sententiae, terrere-
> mur auctoritate censurae. (II,15)

But when he can conquer his sense of affront sufficiently to look
at the argument, he has a telling criticism. Victor seems to think he
has solved the problem of the unbaptized by providing a sort of
second chance for their inclusion in the benefits of the sacraments.
Not really, says Augustine. He has only pushed the problem back
one step farther. Instead of the child's fate being finally dependent
on its baptism, it depends on whether it has an intercessor to offer
the proper prayers after its death. What seems a generous provision
is in fact a cheat, for the child's salvation lies in the hands of humans,
subject to whim and chance; and it is far more cruel to base hope
for the salvation of infants on the capriciousness of fate or of human
decision than on God's judgment (II,21). Augustine's solution,
though it seems hardhearted in applying condemnation to infants,
at least leaves their disposition in the hands of a just and merciful
God.

> [Victor] can find nothing to say about those countless thou-
> sands of infants who are born among unbelievers and die
> among unbelievers. I am not speaking of those whom
> people wished to aid through baptism but could not. I mean
> rather those whose baptism has never occurred to anyone,
> nor will it—for whom no one has offered nor ever will offer
> the sacrifice which [Victor] has decreed should be offered
> even for the unbaptized. (II,21)

That outburst reveals again the agonized questioner of Epistle 166;
Augustine's conclusions have come at a high price.

Victor's suggestion will only vindicate God's justice if the sacrament can be offered on behalf of every child ever born, a clear
impossibility (II,21). /61/ Therefore Augustine begs him to abandon
his effort to tie both sin and regeneration to the flesh (IV,16), /62/
lest God be charged with condemning the innocent either in assign-

ing the soul to flesh in the first place or in subsequently denying the opportunity for remission of sin through the sacraments.

The eleventh error: "Noli credere . . . aliquos eorum, qui sine baptismo Christi ex hac vita migraverint, interim non ire in regnum caelorum, sed in paradisum, postea vero in resurrectione mortuorum etiam ad regni caelorum beatitudinem pervenire." (I, 10; II, 14 and 16; III, 19)

Like the ninth error, this one seeks to make what Augustine considers an unwarranted distinction in terms. Because Jesus on the cross promised "paradise" to the repentant thief,/63/ Victor concludes that this realm is open to the unbaptized, implying its inferiority to the kingdom of heaven.

Augustine exclaims that even Pelagius did not dare to make such an assertion as granting heaven to the unbaptized (III, 19), and it seems that Victor did not offer any proof for the second part. In fact he acknowledges that John 3:5 counts against him but nevertheless invokes "both the result and the working out [*effectum et affectum*] of the divine mercy and foreknowledge" (III, 19). Augustine prefers Pelagius's heretical consistency in granting infants salvation by denying original sin to Victor's compassionate arbitrariness.

Augustine laments that any one of these eleven statements could make a heretic out of Victor (III, 23). That might seem to imply that Victor is scarcely recognizable as a Catholic, but the examination of the errors separately has shown the many interrelationships among them; some follow naturally from others. For example, Victor's reducing the importance of baptism is a logical consequence of his adherence to creationism—a consequence which helps explain why Augustine wished so urgently to hear Jerome's defense of it. But Victor's opinions on sin and the soul would seem to require baptism. One has the feeling that his baptism arguments grow more from tenderheartedness (*misericordia*) than purely intellectual conviction. There is a logical connection between the idea that sin comes through flesh and that sin is expiated through the physical sign of second birth offered in baptism, but Victor looks also for a way outside of baptism since obviously many will be excluded.

Victor's instinct was vindicated by the Church's later solution which found a way to reconcile *misericordia* and Scripture, though not without the provision of a *medius locus*, something Augustine had thought of but rejected./64/

In the first chapter of this dissertation (p. 18 and p. 26) reference was made to Augustine's distinction between *ratio* and *auctoritas*, which he took to mean human reason and the authority of Scripture. The eleven refutations of Victor's arguments rely on both, as the table on page 71 illustrates.

It is clear from this table that Augustine's arguments are fairly evenly divided between *ratio* and *auctoritas*, even where the argument is over a passage of Scripture. The balance reveals Augustine's conviction that reason and faith are complementary—his famous "Credo ut intellegam; intellego ut credam." *De Ordine* II,9,26, an early work, expresses the balance thus: "Tempore auctoritas, re autem ratio prior est." Although *auctoritas* meant Scripture, and Scripture enlightened the reader regarding God's purposes, nevertheless Augustine believed happiness was not possible to one who lived by authority alone.

Over the main issue of the treatise, traducianism vs. creationism, neither reason nor authority could lead to a necessary conclusion. Where both fail, the proper stance, Augustine believes, is suspended judgment, in fact, a *philosopher's* detachment! This is how Augustine comes to spend so much time, in this treatise, on knowledge and ignorance.

The refrain on which Book III is constructed bears some examination. Why the sequence "Noli credere . . . dicere . . . docere"? First, the formula converts what might have been an abstract debate over a philosophical problem into a matter of action. The nature of the soul was one of the standard topics, both pagan and Christian, of scholarly inquiry. Augustine himself had addressed it in two early works written just after his baptism: the *Soliloquies* (386) and *De Quantite Animae* (387). But the direction of his present inquiry is quite different, for it is carried out in response to a challenge to both faith and reason. The early investigations were products of the retreat into contemplative *otium*; this treatise emerges from conflict, and Augustine has a pragmatic aim—the "conversion" of Victor. "Noli credere" warns him not to endanger his own salvation, to change his mind. "Noli dicere, noli docere" point toward the consequences of Victor's errors for church practice.

The order of the commands—*credere, dicere, docere*—has a particular significance in relation to the notion of Christian rhetoric as proclamation. The formula presupposes the chain of receiving and passing on characteristic of Christian community (in the New Testament παραλαβεῖν and παραδοῦναι). One person accepts the

ERROR	REFUTATION FROM REASON	REFUTATION FROM AUTHORITY
1. God made soul from Himself	God would condemn Himself Breath not part of Himself Changeless cannot produce changeable Breath cannot create	"Impious" Genesis creation account Uniqueness of the Son
2. God gives souls continuously	Impossible unless preexistence	Will be an end of giving souls
3. Soul lost merit through being incarnated	Impossible unless preexistence	Preexistence condemned
4. Soul repaired through flesh	Impossible unless preexistence	Unborn have done nothing
5. Soul deserved to be sinful	Impossible unless preexistence	
6. Unbaptized infants are forgiven original sin		No biblical evidence
7. Predestined for baptism might die first	God would predestine what does not happen God would foreknow what does not happen	Impiety to doubt God's foreknowledge and power
8. Wisdom 4:11 applies to unbaptized	Makes unbaptized better off than baptized	Mistaken application of Scripture
9. Some mansions outside kingdom of God	Analogy of earthly king Victor using "kingdom" in different senses	No Biblical evidence for *medius locus*
10. Offer Mass for unbaptized		No precedent Victor's arrogance
11. Separating paradise and kingdom of God	Contradicts original sin	John 3:5

word from another (*credere*), one talks it over inwardly or outwardly (*dicere*), one relays it to the next hearer (*docere*). This public dimension of Augustine's "true philosophy" ensured that he could never really depart from his old profession of rhetor, for there was no end to the work of instruction and persuasion.

NOTES

/1/   DNOA IV,20, cf. Tertullian *De An*. 9,7.

/2/   "Nihil enim si non corpus," *De An*. 7,3. More on this at p. 45 ff.

/3/   *Le Stoïcisme des Pères de l'église de Clément de Rome à Clément d'Alexandrie* (Paris: Éditions du Seuil, 1957), pp. 159–165.

/4/   A detailed history of the "spiritualization" of πνεῦμα is presented by G. Verbeke, *L'Évolution de la doctrine du Pneuma du Stoïcisme à St. Augustin* (Paris: Desclée de Brouwer, 1945).

/5/   *De An*. 5,2. Trans. ANF, vol.3., p. 184, parentheses theirs.

/6/   In describing Tertullian's error in *De Haeresibus 86* (CCL 46, p. 338), Augustine approves of his assertion that the soul is immortal but disapproves of calling it *corpus* and especially of calling God *corpus*. Yet Augustine admits this disapproval does not provide grounds for calling Tertullian a heretic: "nec tamen hinc haereticus dicitur factus." And he understands that Tertullian wishes thereby to assert the reality of God: "sed potuit, ut dixi, propterea putari corpus deum dicere, quia non est nihil, non est inanitas, non est corporis vel animae qualitas, sed ubique totus, et per locorum spatia nulla partitus, in sua tamen natura atque substantia incommutabiliter permanet."

/7/   *Conf*. V,19–20 and VII,1–2. Augustine's metaphor of the giant sponge in *Conf*. VII,7 sounds very like C.S. Lewis's account of the woman whose attempts to conceive of God as a perfect "substance" led her to picture Him as "something like a vast tapioca pudding" (*Miracles*, ch.10).

/8/   See I,5 and II,7. In fact, Christians were still finding it possible to defend the corporeality of the soul for some time after Augustine, see E. Fortin, *Christianisme et culture philosophique au Vième siècle: la querelle de l'âme humaine en Occident* (Paris: Études augustiniennes, 1959).

/9/   PL 33, col. 721–722. FOC translation, vol. 30, p. 9. The second sentence reads, "Si corpus est omnis substantia, vel essentia, vel si quid aptius nuncupatur id quod aliquo modo est in seipso, corpus est anima." Augustine recognizes that the use of "*corpus*" is "a question of reality" ("de re constat," *De Haer. 86*, CCL 46, p. 338) for Tertullian. Augustine asserts God's reality in *Enn. in Ps.* 68/69:5 (CCL 39, p. 905) by using the term "*substantia*" in a way similar to Tertullian's use of "*corpus*": "Quod nulla substantia est nihil omnino est. . . . Substantia ergo aliquid esse est." Augustine adds that then "God is a sort of substance." For Tertullian's terminology, see G.C. Stead, "Divine Substance in Tertullian," JTS 14:1 (April, 1963), pp. 47–67.

/10/ *Ep.* 190,IV,14, FOC transl., vol. 30, p. 279.

/11/ See Verbeke, pp. 20–73. Tertullian names some of these writers and their divisions of the soul in *De An.* 14.

/12/ *Conf.* VII,26. The tripartite division is found in e.g., *Tim.* 30b: νοῦν μὲν ἐν ψυχῇ, ψυχὴν δὲ ἐν σώματι, ξυνιστὰς τὸ πᾶν ξυνετεκταίνετο.

/13/ Later Neoplatonism used the expression ὄχημα τῆς ψυχῆς for the πνεῦμα, the vehicle which surrounds the soul as it descends and takes possession of its body. That picture is the reverse image of Victor's: body-within-soul-within-spirit instead of spirit-within-soul-within-body.

/14/ For earlier Jewish-Christian use of the terms see H.A.A. Kennedy, *Philo's Contribution to Religion* (London: Hodder and Stoughton, 1919). Philo's use of πνεῦμα, ψυχή, and νοῦς is compared with Paul's on pp. 85–95.

/15/ IV,36. The Scriptural texts Augustine means which employ "spirit" in various ways are the following: I Thess. 5:23, Job 7:15, Rom. 7:25, Gal. 5:17, Eph. 4:23, Col. 2:11, I Cor. 14:14, Jn. 19:30, Gen 1:20 and 24, Eccles. 3:21, Gen. 7:21–22, Jn. 4:24, Ps. 148/9:8, Ps. 106/7:25.

/16/ F.J. Thonnard, "'Mens' et 'spiritus,'" BA 22, p. 859, n. 64.

/17/ p. 409.

/18/ Gen. 2:7.

/19/ pp. 223–236.

/20/ For Augustine's Christian realization of this theme, see R. O'Connell, *St. Augustine's Early Theory of Man* and *St. Augustine's Confessions: The Odyssey of Soul*. Etienne Gilson (*The Christian Philosophy of St. Augustine*, trans. L.E.M. Lynch [New York: Random House, 1960]), doubts whether Augustine ever broke entirely with this theory: "everything leads us to believe that he always mistook Plotinus's emanation for the Christian notion of creation" (p. 108).

/21/ "The soul is indeed made by God, but it is not part or nature of God." "God did not make the soul from nothing, but it is from Him in such

74 Eloquence and Ignorance

a way that it emanated from Him." And "Souls are of the same *genus* as God by His gift, not by nature." "You do not think it follows necessarily that the soul is of the nature of God, since even you yourself recognize how impious that would be."

/22/ *De An.* 11.

/23/ Ibid., 22.

/24/ Augustine's treatment of the second error is an example of overstating the opponent's argument.

/25/ "Aux origines," pp. 128–129, n. 50, my trans.

/26/ See BA 48 "La préexistence des âmes," pp. 714–717 and BA 49, "Origine des âmes singulières," pp. 530–534. For the discussion of these points in *De Gen.* see X,2,3: "Ipsa hominis anima in illis operibus [the works of the 6 days] facta est, corporis vero eius in mundo corporeo tamquam in semine ratio." cf. *De Gen.* VII,24,35.

/27/ See R. Nash, *The Light of the Mind*, pp. 81–86; Gilson, *Christian Philosophy of St. Augustine*, pp. 68–75; and R. O'Connell, *St. Augustine's Early Theory of Man*, pp. 146–155. O'Connell's later article "Pre-existence in Augustine's Seventh Letter," REA V (1969), pp. 67–73, was challenged by Gerald J. P. O'Daly, "Did Augustine Ever Believe in the Soul's Pre-existence?" *Augustinian Studies* 5 (1974), pp. 227–235. O'Daly denies that Augustine's early presentation of that opinion implied acceptance.

/28/ See J. Rist, *Plotinus: The Road to Reality* (Cambridge: Cambridge University Press, 1967), especially chapter 9, "The Descent of the Soul."

/29/ *De Princ.* I,8,4; II,9,7; III,3,5.

/30/ TeSelle, p. 264.

/31/ It has been fashionable for some time to blame the Greeks, Plato in particular, for introducing body-soul dualism into Christianity, thereby spoiling the (superior) Hebrew unitary view of humanity. The note in BA 48, pp. 696–697, points out, however, that the equation Greek:Hebrew = dualist:monist is too facile, for even the Hebraic Genesis account—man formed from clay, then animated by the breath of God—presumes some kind of duality in a human being. For all their conviction that the soul is the superior part of the human person and the bearer of the image of God, the writers of the early Church stoutly defended as essential to the faith the doctrine of the resurrection of the *body*, i.e., the unity of the person. The commentator of BA 48 notes a tendency to exaggerate the contrast between Greek dualism and Hebrew monism.

/32/   There is always the temptation to translate Paul's *"corpus peccati"* (Rom. 6:6) and *"corpus mortis huius"* (Rom. 7:24) in a gnostic sense, making the body the cause of sin.

/33/   Rom. 9:11 (RSV), referring to Jacob and Esau and the puzzling verse of the OT, "Jacob I loved, but Esau I hated" (Mal. 1:2–3). Oddly enough, Origen used the same verse in connection with preexistence: "There is no unrighteousness in the fact that Jacob supplanted his brother even in the womb, provided we believe that by reason of his merits in some previous life Jacob had deserved to be loved by God to such an extent as to be worthy of being preferred to his brother" (*De Princ.* II,9,7). See ch.4, n. 5, on preexistence.

/34/   "And so, if the soul, which could not be a sinner, deserved to be a sinner, it still did not remain in sin, since it was prefigured in [the case of] Christ that it must not be in sin, just as it could not be."

/35/   BA 22, p. 298, introduction to DNOA.

/36/   BA 22, p. 315.

/37/   For the difficulties introduced into Western theology by the connotations of the term *"meritum,"* see Burnaby, pp. 235–241.

/38/   Infant baptism is mentioned by Augustine in *De Gen.* X,23,39 as tipping the scales in favor of traducianism, since the Scriptural texts do not give a clear answer. However, his comment there is "What can be said of these arguments is not yet clear to me."

/39/   *Retr.* II,45.

/40/   The Romans verses are quoted repeatedly in all of Augustine's anti-Pelagian works, see Thonnard "Le sens de Rom. V,12 en son contexte" in BA 23, pp. 734–740, another instance of a translation difficulty affecting a doctrinal point. Augustine explicates this passage more fully in *Contra Duas Epistolas Pelagianorum* IV,7 (PL 44, PNF 1st ser., 5). More texts supporting Augustine's doctrine of original sin are found in *De Nuptiis et Concupiscentia* (PL 44, PNF 1st ser., 5) written 419–420, ch. 50. Jn. 3:5, "Unless one is born again of water and the Spirit . . ." appears numerous places in DNOA. Elsewhere (*De Peccatorum Meritis et Remissione, et de Baptismo Parvulorum* I,68) (PL 44, PNF 1st ser., 5) Augustine adds to the Scriptural and ecclesiastical evidence for original sin the observable state of pitiable ignorance and weakness in babies: "This great infirmity of the flesh clearly, in my opinion, points to a something, whatever it may be, that is penal" (PNF).

/41/   In *De Nupt. et Conc.* Augustine bolsters his assertion that the Church has always baptized infants by citing Ambrose and Cyprian (ch. 51). Pelagius had accused Augustine of falling back into Manichaeanism in speaking of human nature as universally corrupted through Adam's sin. For a collection of texts and commentaries on the early Christian understanding of baptism, see J.-Ch. Didier, *Faut-il baptiser les enfants?* (Paris: Éditions du Cerf, 1967); also the sources used in the debate between J. Jeremias (*Infant Baptism in the First Four Centuries* [Philadelphia: Westminster, 1960] and *The Origins of Infant Baptism* [Naperville, Ind.: Allenson, 1963]).

/42/   *Augustine of Hippo*, p. 385.

/43/   DNOA II,17. Cf. CD XXI,24, written c. 425. See also p. 63.

/44/   *Ep.* 186, dated mid–417: "I will have mercy on whom I will have mercy."

/45/   *Ep.* 186. See P. Fredriksen, "Augustine's Early Interpretation of Paul," Ph.D. dissertation, Princeton University, 1979, pp. 239–247, and TeSelle, pp. 323–324, on the progress of Augustine's thought.

/46/   *Opus Impf.* I,48, seq., trans. P. Brown, *Augustine of Hippo*, p. 391.

/47/   Burnaby observes that Augustine nearly always treats "love of God" as an objective genitive and almost never as a subjective genitive, p. 99. When he writes on I Tim. 2:4, "God would have all men to be saved," Augustine extracts from this straightforward statement, by a tortuous reasoning process, that all who are saved are so by the will of God. See also pp. 238–241 of John Rist's article "Augustine on Free Will and Predestination" in *Augustine: A Collection of Critical Essays*, ed. R.A. Markus (New York: Anchor Books, 1972).

/48/   See above p. 60 and note 41.

/49/   The passage on the thief in I,11 is rhetorically remarkable, see chapter 5, pp. 123–125.

/50/   *De Diversis Quaestionibus LXXXIII* (PL 40), *De Baptismo* (PL 43, PNF 1st ser., 4).

/51/   F.J. Thonnard, "Les deux états de la nature humaine, 'intègre' puis 'corrompue,' et la grace du Christ," BA 21, n. 53, pp. 614–622. "Les 'limbes' des enfants morts sans baptême," BA 22, n. 34, pp. 779–782. "'Damnatio' et le sort des enfants morts sans baptême,' BA 22, n. 35, pp. 782–788.

/52/   *Conf.* III,12.

/53/   Augustine took issue with Cicero over God's foreknowledge vs. free will in CD V,9. Cicero denied that both could exist and chose free will, "and thus," says Augustine, "wishing to make men free he makes them sacrilegious. But the religious mind chooses both, confesses both, and maintains both by the faith of piety."

/54/   In much the same way as he pressed Victor's second error, interpreting it in a heretical sense. See pp. 53–55 above.

/55/   See above, p. 62.

/56/   *De Pecc. Mer.* I,58, dated 412 (PL 44).

/57/   Ibid., I,26–27. "Except you eat my flesh and drink my blood, you shall have no life in you."

/58/   "Baptism," *Catholic Encyclopedia*, 1907 ed.

/59/   "'Damnatio' et le sort des enfants morts sans baptême," BA 22, n. 35, p. 786. The role of Christ as Savior for those outside the Church as well as in it is affirmed by the *Constitutio de Ecclesia* of Vatican II (1964).

/60/   Viz., the story told in II Macc. 12:39–45. The analogy would hold true, says Augustine, only if the men had been uncircumcized, since circumcision is the Old Testament equivalent of baptism.

/61/   To refer again to the 1907 *Catholic Encyclopedia*, one sees an ambivalent solution in conservative, pre-Vatican-II theology. Under "Dead, prayers for," the Encyclopedia says one can offer prayers for those unbaptized persons "who may have died in a state of grace," and a priest may offer private, but not public, Mass for such persons.

/62/   See p. 60 above.

/63/   Lk. 23:43.

/64/   See above, p. 65.

CHAPTER 3

AUGUSTINE AND

"KNOWING WHAT YOU DO NOT KNOW"/1/

It might have seemed sufficient for Augustine to answer Victor's points one by one and then to move on to more important controversies. Instead, half of *De Natura et Origine Animae* is preoccupied with the theme of knowing and not knowing. Book II takes hold of Peter's words of praise for Victor, that Victor taught him what he did not know before, and obstinately asks what Peter has learned. Book IV turns the question inward: What do we know and what can we learn about ourselves? And the whole treatise is haunted by the problem of ignorance.

Augustine perhaps sees in this self-confident young challenger a mirror of his own "swelling pride" as a young, successful orator. As Cicero's *Hortensius* had once converted Augustine from the desire for success to the search for wisdom, so Augustine tries to direct Victor away from the *vanitas* of rhetorical cleverness, novelty, and public applause. By the demonstration of human ignorance and limitations, Augustine aims to teach Victor a more appropriate humility. Yet Augustine has rejected with equal vigor the sceptic's position that we can know nothing for certain. Indeed, *Contra Academicos*, a protest against scepticism, was the very first thing Augustine wrote after his conversion. Between the poles of *superbia* (the presumption of complete knowledge) and scepticism (the denial of any certainty) there must be a middle ground characterized by both *humilitas* and an active intelligence.

Plainly Augustine wishes to defend himself against the charge of irresponsible ignorance, but Book IV is too long and too elaborate to be merely the reaction of wounded self-esteem. His purpose is rather, I believe, to curb Victor's pride,/2/ and it is interesting that he chooses maxims from classical literature rather than Scripture to

accomplish his purpose: Victor must come to know what he does
not know and to know himself. Failure will endanger his soul.

That we cannot know for certain the origin of the soul is one
particular instance of our limitation. Augustine shifts the accent in
Victor's question so that it becomes a question about knowing. Victor asks: What do we know about the *soul?* Augustine acknowledges
with Victor the soul's origin from God but then changes the question to, What do we *know* about the soul? Victor had wanted to add
some particular theories about the soul to the body of Christian
dogma. Augustine wants to mark off the territory first, to ask where
knowledge is possible and where not, to justify his refusal to claim
certain knowledge. This chapter will examine how Augustine does
this.

Behind him lie two traditions, Greek philosophy (as transmit-
ted through Roman education) and the Bible, both of which have a
good deal to say about knowing and not knowing. For Augustine the
Bible is the ultimate authority, not that it is to be preferred to reason but that it will confirm the findings of true philosophy or at least
provide clues about those things not accessible to reason at all. It
helps to define what we can know and not know and thus assists us
in finding where reason may profitably be used. His confidence that
reason and Scripture will not conflict because they are complementary ways of approaching a single truth shows up in his handling of
Victor's arguments and also, at about this same period in his life, in
his respectful comments on philosophy in *City of God* VIII. Tertullian's dark suspicions about philosophy and Jerome's celebrated
nightmare about being judged a Ciceronian rather than a Christian
reflect an uneasiness about philosophy which is less apparent in
Augustine./3/

DNOA can be looked at as an example of the combining of the
philosophical and Biblical ways of thinking about knowledge. Augustine's model in his questioning is plainly Socrates, the man who,
as Augustine puts it in *City of God* (VIII,3), "detected the ignorance
of these overweening fellows that build castles on their own knowledge, either in this, confessing his own ignorance, or dissembling
his understanding." Augustine's final refusal to take sides regarding
the origin of the soul resembles the Socratic *aporia* (though his mo-
tive for leaving the principal question unresolved in the end is quite
different. See p. 85 below). Throughout three of the books of the
treatise one meets phrases that echo the Socrates of Plato's early
dialogues, for example:

1) . . . ne cogatur insipientiam profiteri, dum veretur ignorantiam confiteri (I,16).
2) Nunc autem nescio nec me pudet fateri nescire quod nescio (I,25). (Cf. Cic. *Tusculan Disputations* I,25,60.)
3) non audeo docere quod nescio . . . (I,26).
4) Moneo ut quod nescit se nescire fateatur, neque id quod nondum didicit docere moliatur (I,26).
5) . . . ne incognitis fidant et temere audeant affirmare quod nesciunt . . . (I,30).
6) Melius est enim homini fateri se nescire quod nescit (I,34).
7) . . . quid per illum veritatis acceperis. Vellem . . . quid te docuerit me doceres (II,1).
8) . . . quid ab eo didiceris nosse cupio, ut, si iam id sciebam, gratuler pro te, si autem nesciebam, discam per te (II,2).
9) Aliud est discere, aliud videri sibi didicisse (II,10).
10) Ego autem et me doctissimum ac peritissimum nescio, immo vero me non esse certissime scio (IV,1).
11) . . . quia existimasti te scire quod nescis (IV,1).
12) . . . ne pro cognitis incognita praesumendo ad veritatem pervenire non possis (IV,11).
13) Videas profecto quantum tibi profuisset si scisses nescire quod nescis, et quantum tibi prosit si vel nunc scias. . . . Intellege quid non intellegas, ne totum non intellegas, et noli despicere hominem qui, ut veraciter intellegat quod non intellegit, hoc se non intellegere intellegit (IV,15).
14) . . . qui neque negant se scire quod sciunt et confitentur se nescire quod nesciunt (IV,15).
15) Si vis esse victor erroris, nec te, quando aliquid nescis, existimes scire, sed, ut scias, disce nescire (IV,38). (Note the pun on Victor's name.)

One could add to this list the repeated question of Book II, "What did Victor teach you that you did not know?" as another instance of Socratic method; by this ironic reiteration Augustine is, as he said of his predecessor, "either confessing his own ignorance or dissembling his understanding" (CD VIII,3), and pressing his adversary towards an admission of ignorance.

In the above statements Augustine operates with the same classifications as the Socrates of Plato's *Apology*: those who are ashamed to confess their ignorance, those who seem to know but do not really, those who confuse the known with the unknown, and those who know only that they do not know. The one whom Delphi called the wisest of men concluded that he was so only because he knew that he knew nothing. Augustine seems to commend a similar suspension of judgment to his youthful opponent, and by using the vocabulary and ironic questioning associated with Socrates, he gives his approval to a pagan model for Christian debate. Clarity requires some explanation here of what is meant by "Socrates." Obviously it is not germane to go into the "Socratic problem." Rather one needs to ask whether we can legitimately apply the term "Socratic" to what Augustine does, whether we can assume that he has him in mind.

Scholars are now substantially agreed that Augustine's acquaintance with Greek culture relied on secondary sources./4/ Although in the *Confessions* (VII,13) Augustine refers to his reading of some *"libri platonici,"* scholars have long acknowledged that this cannot mean the dialogues of Plato./5/ His familiarity with the *Phaedo, Symposium, Meno,* and *Republic* seems limited to a few famous quotations. He makes more extended use of the *Timaeus* in his section on the creation in *City of God,* but Hagendahl finds no evidence that the Greek text lies behind his references; rather Cicero's translation seems to be his source, and TeSelle doubts that even here Augustine had more than an abridged version./6/ Hagendahl's volume of quotations, correspondences, and sources leaves no doubt that "Cicero was Augustine's main source of knowledge of earlier Greek philosophy."/7/

Quotations from Cicero's *Academica* cover several pages in Hagendahl's study, so one can safely assume that Augustine knew the description of Socrates found in *Academica Posteriora* I,4,15– 18, where Socrates has the following characteristics:

1) Instead of investigating cosmic phenomena, he studied the objects of everyday life.
2) His main concern was to live well.
3) He affirmed nothing himself but only refuted the assertions of others.
4) He claimed ignorance except of the fact that he was ignorant, and herein he was superior to other men. Apollo's commendation was for this reason alone.
5) He encouraged all to study virtue.
6) Plato's systematizing, according to Cicero, abandoned Socratic doubt and *aporia,* and Socrates would not have approved of what either the Academics or the Peripatetics made of his teaching.

The *Tusculan Disputations,* also very well known to Augustine, confirms the first point, that Socrates "called philosophy down from heaven and established it in the cities, introduced it even into private houses, and compelled it to investigate life, and manners, and what was good and evil among men" (V,4). By his scepticism Cicero claimed to be following the method most true to Socrates' own, arguing "so as to conceal my own opinion, while I deliver others from their errors, and so discover what has the greatest appearance of probability in every question."

Looking at the Latin text of the fourth point above, one recognizes the vocabulary and mode of expression of Augustine's phrases about knowing and not-knowing:

> . . . ita disputet ut nihil adfirmet ipse, refellat alios, nihil se scire dicat nisi id ipsum, eoque praestare ceteris, quod illi quae nesciant scire se putent, ipse se nihil scire, id unum sciat, ob eamque rem se arbitrari ab Apolline omnium sapientissimum esse dictum, quod haec esset una omnis sapientia non arbitrari sese scire quod nesciat./8/

That is not to say that Augustine had in mind a particular passage of Cicero as he wrote DNOA but only that this sort of play on knowing and not-knowing was part of the Latin tradition about Socrates, whether Augustine took it from Cicero or simply from the fund of common opinion. (The speaker's citation of the proverb about "the pig teaching Minerva" at the beginning of *Academica Posteriora* [I,5] indicates that the above-mentioned characteristics of Socrates' career were commonplaces in Cicero's time.)

To point out, then, where Augustine's method and vocabulary are "Socratic" is not to press any particular theory about the historical Socrates or his relation to Plato's dialogues, but merely to observe that, like the Socrates known to Latin tradition, Augustine plays ironically with the ideas of knowing and not-knowing, admits his own ignorance, and occasionally harries his opponents.

Is there any similarity in the reasons behind Socrates' *aporia* and Augustine's suspension of judgment? When Socrates asks a listener, What is justice? (or piety, or courage), he is always dissatisfied with the reply because the answers only name instances of justice and do not define the thing itself. But if we did not know what justice is, we could not recognize or agree on instances of it; yet clearly we do. Our way of speaking and reasoning is a clue pointing to the reality of justice (piety, courage), Plato's Form of justice./9/ Socrates aims to clear away ignorance, to make it possible for truth to be seen, but his modest claim is that he is a midwife, not a teacher. Hence he does not lay out a theory but drives his adversary to where truth may be evident to him, then stands back.

Augustine holds a similar view on the possibility of teaching. The thesis of *De Magistro*, which he never abandoned, is that Truth is the real teacher; a human instructor can only guide. Augustine's opening chapter to Peter (DNOA II,1) demonstrates that he still holds that theory: "I praise you for honoring your teacher, not a human being but that Truth which deigned to speak to you through him." In I,19, Augustine twice in speaking of the Old Testament meaning of "spirit" quotes the verse "aspiratio autem omnipotentis quae docet," which links the function of teaching especially to the Holy Spirit. At IV,13 he invokes the Spirit: "Doceat me quando voluerit [Deus]. . . . Sed ille hoc me doceat Spiritus qui altitudines Dei scrutatur, non homo qui spiritum nescit unde uter inflatur."/10/ Where Victor has quoted the teaching of the Apostle Paul, Augustine reminds him that the apostle's teaching ultimately comes from God: "'Disce,' inquit, 'ecce apostolus docet.' Discam plane, si apostolus docet—non enim nisi Deus per apostolum docet"(I,26). In another passage (III,18) he again reminds Victor who the true teacher is: ". . . via quam Christus humilis se ipsum esse docuit." Augustine's irony in Book II revolves around Peter's misapprehension concerning teachers. In praising his protégé for "teaching him what he did not know," Peter has, in Augustine's view, elevated Victor to an impossibly exalted, if not downright blasphemous position. Augustine's many sarcastic references in Book II to Victor as a teacher of learned men are more than just pique at a young man's presumption; they are warnings to Victor and Peter that they have got the whole picture wrong. Rather than setting Victor up as a teacher, they should acknowledge that the human role is merely to point toward, to remind, in Socratic terms, to act the midwife's part (II,6a). What Victor and Peter took for teaching and learning was, in fact, an illusion: "aliud est discere, aliud videri sibi didicisse. Si ergo te didicisse arbitraris quod adhuc nescis, non plane didicisti, sed temere credidisti quod libenter audisti . . ." (II,10). Better Peter should unlearn anything he has learned from Victor: "Volo ut quod didiceras ipse dediscas" (II,5).

Augustine's questioning of Victor in IV,3–10 follows a Socratic pattern as he demonstrates the folly of assuming one knows all about oneself. Like Socrates, he confesses his ignorance of what his opponent claims to know easily, in this case the origin of the soul. Like Socrates, he shows that his opponent's "knowledge" is far from reliable or certain and that his analogies are inappropriate. In short he makes his adversary look foolish while offering no solution of his own.

There is a third way in which one could say that Augustine

follows a Socratic model, but again one must ask what conception of Socrates Augustine held. When Socrates "called philosophy down from heaven," was he transforming the *approach* to the study of the nature of things by starting from that which lay closest to hand, viz., man's own ideas? Or was he abandoning cosmic speculation altogether in favor of practical wisdom? The contrast is roughly that between Plato's Socrates and Xenophon's. There is evidence in an earlier work of Augustine's, *De Quantitate Animae* (c. 388), that he considers the more modest task to be the one enjoined by Greek philosophy. At the very beginning of that treatise, Evodius complains that Augustine has been putting him off with "that Greek saw which tells us not to seek what is beyond our powers." /11/ If that maxim represents Greek thought to Augustine, he has another proof that true philosophy and Scripture will not prove contradictory, for the "Greek saw" is nearly identical to Sirach 3:21–22, a frequent text in DNOA IV: "Do not inquire into what is too high for you or search out what is beyond your strength, but what the Lord commands you, think upon this always." The expression is not, however, necessarily an anti-intellectual one, an excuse not to bother one's head with mathematics or astronomy; it may also be seen as a reminder of man's place in the cosmos, a warning against hubris, an acknowledgement of the gods' transcendence in relation to human limitations.

Is it for either of these two reasons that Augustine leaves the origin-of-the-soul question open? Both enter into his consideration. In IV,14 he shows the question's secondary importance in comparison with the question of the soul's destiny. In II,7 he leaves it to those who have the leisure or inclination for "subtle disputes," a hint of the characteristically Roman impatience with pure speculation. If the dispute has got no practical application, why bother with it? But the warning against hubris is present too. Augustine's outburst of wonder at man's complexity (IV,8) reminds his readers of the insuperable gap between divine and human understanding.

Yet there is a new and plainly un-Socratic factor in Augustine's refusal to give the answer: not just his desire that Victor should find it for himself, not just the futility of idle speculation or the danger of trespassing on divine territory, but the presence of revelation and Catholic dogma. There is now a new given, not only the one evident from the way human language works or the way we reason, but one that comes from the divine side. For Augustine that revealed truth includes a universal and hereditary weight of sin, attested to by

Romans 5:18 ("Through the offense of one man judgment came upon all men unto condemnation") and by the Church's practice of infant baptism. If God creates souls new for each human being, as Victor asserts, how will one avoid attributing to Him the creation of an imperfect or deformed entity such as revelation tells us the fallen soul is? At this point the debate has moved into territory where, to Augustine's mind, there *is* certainty.

"Knowing what you do not know," then, in this treatise means recognizing that an apparently perfectly reasonable theory about how humans get "ensouled" conflicts with two pieces of certain knowledge: (1) that all that God creates is "very good" and (2) that humans are born sinful. The only solution Augustine sees is to back off from the theory and leave it in the category of the unknown until the conflict can be resolved. Augustine knows that he is unable to resolve it; he has tried for years./12/ He "knows what he does not know," and on this particular question he "knows that he knows nothing." Victor still thinks he knows something about this question, but his knowledge is illusory; he needs to learn what he does not know. Augustine has hopes that a more ingenious mind than his may some day solve the problem, but he is ruefully certain that Victor is not his man (e.g., I,33; II,17; IV,5).

We have looked at the classical antecedents for Augustine's handling of the theme of knowing and not knowing in this treatise. Let us compare that with the ideas he inherits from Scripture. I have already mentioned a passage from Sirach which figures prominently in Book IV: "Do not inquire into what is too high for you or search out what is beyond your strength; but what the Lord commands you, think upon this always." /13/ The same theme appears in Psalm 139:6, which Augustine quotes in IV,12: "Your knowledge is too marvelous for me; it is too strong; I cannot attain it." That divine things should surpass human understanding is no less a classical idea than a Biblical one. Besides the Greek proverb mentioned above, /14/ one could point to approving references from patristic writing to Plato's *Timaeus*: "But the father and maker of all this universe is past finding out, and even if we found him, to tell of him to all men would be impossible."/15/ Perfect knowledge is not a human possibility in either classical or Biblical thought; neither Semele nor Moses can look on the glory of God and live. Augustine says elsewhere/16/ that being, life, and understanding coincide only in God Himself; in other words, perfect knowledge is an attribute of God alone.

This is not to say that Augustine wishes to cut off certain topics from human inquiry; rather his aim is to check Victor's temerity (a word Augustine uses often about his adversary) and urge upon him a more modest attitude in debate. Defining "the things that are too high" is not such an obvious task. Augustine spends some effort in discussing what that verse means so that Victor will not again rush into some simplistic conclusion. At first glance one might think the warning applies to speculation about God and the universe in contrast to earthly things. Not so, says Augustine. The odd truth is that we know in some ways more about God and about the planets than we do about ourselves and our earthly companions: "Some among the works of God are more difficult to understand than God Himself insofar as He can be understood. For example, we have learned that God is a Trinity; but how many sorts of animals He created . . . we still do not know (unless perchance you have already found this out)" (IV,6). "Why have I no need of art to know that there is a sun and moon and other stars in the sky, but I need art to know how I initiate the movement of my finger . . . ?" (IV,7). Victor has fallen into the trap of assuming that knowledge is a matter of simple distance, that what is nearest to us is easiest to know and what is farthest from us the hardest.

On the contrary Scripture assumes that God *can* be known from His creation. Augustine quotes a verse from a chapter that marvels at human obtuseness in the face of the natural evidence for God: "For if they had the power to know so much that they could investigate the world, how did they fail to find sooner the Lord of these things?"/17/ Here a spirit of inquiry is what leads one to faith.

In a characteristic example of his ability to turn an opponent's argument against him, Augustine picks up Victor's citation of a story in the Book of Maccabees to show that Victor has oversimplified the question of what we can know. As a heroic mother watches her sons suffering hideous tortures, she exhorts them to hope for God's restoration of their life:

"I do not know how you were formed in my womb, for I gave you neither breath nor soul (*spiritum et animam*), nor did I form the visage or the limbs of each one of you. But God who created the world and everything in it, who made the human race and who finds out the conduct of all, He will restore to you again breath and soul by His great mercy." /18/

Victor had used this passage to support his contention that the soul is made by God for each new person. Augustine denies that the text necessarily eliminates a traducianist interpretation—no one denies that God makes the soul; the argument is over how He makes it—but he commends the mother for her confession of ignorance. Victor ought to imitate her. Obviously she knows that she has conceived her sons from her husband; likewise she knows that God gave them life. What she does not know is not some great cosmic question but something that pertains to human life, the life within her own body at that. This again shows that what is "too high" for us is not necessarily some divine matter but may be what lies within us.

The virtue which appeals to Augustine in the mother of the Maccabean youths is her humility concerning her own knowledge. /19/ Victor's arrogance (IV,15) in the face of the mystery of the soul's origin violates Scripture's warnings that the wisdom of man and the wisdom of God are not the same. "The foolishness of God is wiser than men; and the weakness of God is stronger than men."/20/ In an early work, the opening of *De Doctrina Christiana*, Augustine connects this verse with the Incarnation: "Wisdom Himself saw fit to make Himself congruous with such infirmity as ours"; and then links it to the elegant paradox that "We were trapped by the wisdom of the serpent; we are freed by the foolishness of God."/21/ This paradoxical quality of knowledge, the consciousness that it looks different from God's side than from man's side, divides Christian from classical thinking. Although both classical and Christian traditions claim a kinship between God and man that makes some real knowledge possible, although both counsel a prudent humility toward divine mysteries,/22/ all the Christian fathers acknowledge the *unexpected* quality of God's revelation in the Incarnation: unexpected that God should act from His side, and unexpected that He should choose humility, ignorance, and poverty./23/

Augustine speaks of this contrast between classical and Christian conceptions of wisdom specifically in *Confessions* VII,14, where he compares the "books of the Platonists" with what he has read in Scripture and concludes: "You have hidden these things from the wise and have revealed them to little ones."/24/ To know what one does not know is prudent not only in the Socratic sense of escaping self-delusion, but in the Christian sense of avoiding the fatal confusion of human with divine wisdom and recognizing that God in the Incarnation turns human conceptions of knowledge upside down. Hence to take pride in one's knowledge is the same sort of risk for the Christian that hubris is to the Greek; a human being does not know the mind of God.

Pride also violates the central command of Christianity, namely the command to love. "Scientia inflat, caritas aedificat."/25/ Just before his trip to Mauretania Caesariensis which would bring him in touch with Optatus' inquiries about the origin of the soul,/26/ Augustine used this text in a treatise against the Pelagians, *De Gratia Christi*./27/ In using the analogy of a man inflating a balloon (*uter*) to explain his concept of the soul's insufflation by God (III,4–6), Victor gives the Bishop a golden opportunity to use the same verse against him. Augustine complains that Victor has not even managed to describe that mundane action accurately but has puffed up both himself and his hearers:

> Sed potes hoc facillime discere, si hoc potius velis quam tua dicta, quia iam dicta sunt, non inflans utrem, sed inflatus ipse defendere et auditores tuos, quos veris rebus aedificare debes, inani strepitu ventosi sermonis inflare. (III,5)

The necessary relationship of love and knowledge is stated in, for example, *De Doctrina Christiana* I,40: "whoever thinks that he understands the divine Scriptures or any part of them so that [his understanding] does not build the double love of God and of our neighbor does not understand it at all."/28/ And further, in *De Catechizandis Rudibus* I,4, Augustine sets out God's love as the chief thing any Christian instructor must try to teach. Probably, though, Augustine's rebuke to Victor for his pride is aimed particularly at the kind of misplaced self-assurance shown by the gnostic sects still operating at this time. Augustine refers by name to the Priscillianists as holding a doctrine about the merits of a preexistent soul similar to the one Victor promotes (III,9). It is likely that the priest Peter had been influenced by Priscillianism in Spain, and Augustine counted the letter 190 to Optatus as one of his anti-Priscillianist writings. Augustine had his own experience with gnostic ideas from his career as a Manichaean before his conversion. The tenet common to gnostic thought, that some special knowledge distinguishes the true believers from the rabble, fostered the sort of pride shown by Victor and ignored the rule of love. Augustine's constant dealings with ordinary people as a preacher and a day-to-day settler of disputes and administrative business made him impatient with that kind of pride. He tells Victor (III,1), "You will undoubtedly be a wise man if only you do not consider yourself so, and if you piously, humbly, and earnestly beseech from that One who makes men wise that you may be so." Van der Meer observes:

> It was wholly alien to Augustine to seek to achieve some higher *gnosis* for himself and to preach some kind of vulgarized religion to his people. He knew no ranks in the school of God, and if there was one thing that he really considered vulgar, it was not popular religion but the whole idea of *gnosis*./29/

Marrou also comments on "Augustine's profound respect for ordinary people in contrast to the elitism of antiquity."/30/

I have already mentioned the new factor of revealed authority which influences the Christian idea of what can be known (above pp. 85–86). There are truths necessary for the life of a Christian which cannot be known except through revelation; Augustine names some in IV,14, viz., the resurrection of the body and everlasting life, and the rebirth, renewal, and eternal blessedness of the soul in Christ: "Haec . . . nullo modo nosse valeremus, nisi divinis crederemus eloquiis." Victor's pride, Augustine continues, prevented him from acknowledging the complexity of knowing and kept him from charity; now, although he quotes Scripture liberally hoping to prove his arguments, his pride prevents him from hearing what Scripture says plainly. While trying to establish the salvation of unbaptized infants, he ignores what "Truth Itself thunders through the mouth of Him in whom it is embodied" (II,17). And since the practice of the Church maintains the witness of Scripture down to the present, Victor should recognize that authority as well. "Novel" becomes a pejorative word, and Augustine applies it to Victor's suggestion of offering Mass for the unbaptized dead (II,15; III,18). What is new is likely to be wrong. Undoubtedly the heaviest reminder Augustine gives Victor of the Church's authority is that stern refrain at the beginning of nearly every chapter of Book III: "Noli credere nec dicere nec docere . . . si vis esse catholicus."

The classical formulae on "knowing what you do not know" and the demands of Scriptural and ecclesiastical authority are juxtaposed most strikingly in Book IV,15–16./31/ Knowing what one does not know will keep one from speaking against the Catholic faith, will curb arrogance, and will guard against the misinterpretation of Scripture. Socrates himself might well appreciate the irony that his phrases have here become an exhortation to humility in the face of authority; whatever the accusations against the philosopher were, they never included humility. At the end of chapter 15, although the classical formulae are quoted to represent what the Biblical passage about cattle does *not* mean, nevertheless it is another occasion for Augustine to recommend sober self-knowledge. He does, in fact, connect the formula with a Biblical allusion in the last clause, viz., II Cor. 12:9: "nam virtus in infirmitate perficitur."/32/ In chapter 16 it is the ecclesiastical official speaking in the concern that heretics should not profit from disputes within the Church (Jerome had expressed the same anxiety in Epistle 172 to Augustine as they discussed the origin of the soul). In the end the *occulta opera Dei* remain so.

The appeal to Catholic authority has a special emphasis in Victor's case because he is newly won over to the Church from a Donatist sect (I,2). His continuing admiration for the schismatic bishop Vincentius, his claim even that the old man inspired the material of his book through a dream (III,2), strikes Augustine as a symptom of insincerity in Victor's conversion. His pretense, if such it is, will keep him from real understanding: "If you think him holy and just, you are lost by communing with Catholics. For plainly you only pretend to be a Catholic if you are of the same mind as that one whom you admire. And you know how it is written [in Scripture] with terrible words: 'The Holy Spirit of Wisdom will flee from the pretender.'" The contrast between a feigned Catholic and a real one is expressed in terms of knowledge later and linked again with the Biblical text that strength is made perfect in weakness: "I shall not cease to warn you . . . to acknowledge rather our common weakness in which strength is made perfect, lest by presuming to know what you do not know, you should be unable to arrive at the truth" (IV,11). A similar warning goes to Peter in II,23 not to be "wise against truth" (*adversus veritatem sapis*).

But even where the appeals to the authority of Scripture and the Church are the most uncompromising, it is clear that Augustine never considers them as demands to abandon inquiry, for faith and knowledge are complementary. "Authority demands faith and prepares man for reason. Reason leads him on to knowledge and understanding. But reason is not entirely useless to authority; it helps in considering what authority is to be accepted."/33/ Each time Augustine repeats the "*noli credere*" formula, he bases his disagreement on Biblical evidence together with the close inquiry of reason,/34/ a pattern which he commends to Victor "so that you may profitably use this great gift of disputation which God has given you for the

edification, not the destruction, of sound and healthy doctrine"
(III,21).

The problem with the origin of the soul is that neither independent human reason nor divine revelation gives a certain answer.
Therefore the choice is not knowledge versus ignorance but rather
advertising one's ignorance versus confessing it. How much better,
then, to withhold judgment on the problem.

> Quanto melius tenet de origine animae cunctationem
> meam, ne audeat affirmare quod nec humana ratione con-
> prehendit nec divina auctoritate defendit, ne cogatur insi-
> pientiam profiteri, dum veretur ignorantiam confiteri.
> (I,16)

In a slightly later work, Augustine again uses the Socratic phrase to
differentiate ignorance from error:

> It does not follow that a person who is ignorant of a thing
> must then and there fall into error. He errs only when he
> thinks he knows what he does not know, for he accepts what
> is false as true, and herein lies the essence of error./35/

While the constant appeal to the authority of normative writings is a Christian innovation in the search for knowledge, it would
be inaccurate to say that the classical spirit lacked any notion of
appealing to authority, and simplistic to contrast classical and Christian approaches as illustrating free inquiry versus thought control.
What Augustine means by "faith" is often quite like Plato"s ὀρθὴ
δόξα,/36/ and the Bishop had no more patience with an unexamined faith than the Greeks with the unexamined life. His phrase *per
corporalia ad incorporalia*/37/ does not imply a rejection of the *corporalia*. DNOA illustrates plainly his fascination with the medical
discoveries of his time (IV,6), his interest in dreams (IV,25–26; 34–
35), and his approval of observation (IV,4) and experiment (IV,18) as
reliable ways of reaching conclusions. He shows some annoyance at
Victor's lack of attention to the process of inflating a balloon; if one
is going to use an analogy, one ought at least to have the facts
straight (IV,4). He taunts him with preferring fine book-learning to
commonsense observation:

> Et tamen hoc litteratus homo atque facundus utique nescie-
> bas, quando credebas et dicebas et scribebas et in conventu
> multitudinis conrogatae legebas ex natura nostra nos utrem
> inflare, et in natura nostra nos minus nihil habere, cum hoc

unde faciamus facillime posses, non divinas et humanas pa-
ginas perscrutando, sed in te advertendo nosse cum velles.
/38/

He even scolds him for dragging in Biblical testimonies where unassisted human reason would do the job equally well:

> Just as you do not need to read me anything for me to know
> that I am alive (For my own nature makes it impossible for
> me not to know this), so also why do you produce prooftexts
> from Scripture on this subject [the origin of the soul] for me
> to believe if this is also something we know by nature?
> (IV,14)

Just so in *De Libero Arbitrio* (II,7–27) Augustine assumed that even
the existence of God could be proved through reason without re-
course to Scripture, and in *De Catechizandis Rudibus* he constantly
acknowledged the necessity of beginning one's teaching with things
the students could see for themselves. Augustine never criticizes
Victor for putting too much weight on human reason; his error lies
in over-simplifying the issues and reasoning clumsily.

Victor is not only mistaken about the nature of knowledge; he
is also wrong about the objects of knowledge. Here again oversim-
plification muddles his arguments, and a kind of naive literalism,
for he is unable to conceive of anything being an object of knowledge which does not have a body or a name or a visible form. For
example, in adopting Tertullian's belief that the soul is corporeal
and combining that with Paul's reference to man as body, soul, and
spirit (I Thess. 5:23), he comes up with a picture of man that resembles a Russian doll, with the soul and spirit neatly jelled (*ge-
lante substantia . . . conglobatum*, IV,20) one inside the other.
Nevertheless, Victor insists, the soul has no sex. Augustine has
some rather droll comments on the absurdity of that qualification
(IV,32–33).

Victor has made no distinctions whatsoever in kinds of knowledge; so Augustine must give him a short course in IV,31:

> Since, therefore, there is one [faculty] in the soul by which
> we perceive real bodies (which we do with the five senses
> of our body), another by which, apart from [our senses] we
> discern the things that are like bodies but not bodies (in-
> cluding the apprehension of ourselves as not otherwise than
> like bodies), and another by which we grasp even more
> surely and steadily things which are neither bodies nor like-

nesses of bodies, such as faith, hope, love, which have no
color or extension or similar quality; on which of these [fac-
ulties] should we spend more time or, so to speak, be more
familiar, where we are to be renewed in the knowledge of
God after the image of Him who created us? Is is not in that
one which I put in third place?

Augustine fears Peter may share this same misguided literalism,
when in II,3 he asks: "Did you, a man of such venerable age and
rank, really think, before you heard him, that the sense by which
we distinguish white and black (which even the sparrows see in
common with us) and that by which we judge right from wrong . . .
are one and the same thing?"

Victor has attempted to argue the soul's corporeality from the
fact that Scripture assigns names to Lazarus and Abraham in the
story of the Rich Man (Lk. 16:19–37) and speaks of "Abraham's
bosom." Augustine reminds him of the spiritual realities which have
names yet no describable physical forms: love, joy, peace, etc.
(IV,22). "Abraham's bosom" is no more to be taken literally than the
Psalmist's taking "the wings of a dove," not to mention the problem
of serious overcrowding. (It is surely with tongue in cheek that Augustine accuses Victor of trying to raise a laugh!) Besides, if there
can be no recognition without bodies, how could one be said to
know God (IV,21)? Victor has himself admitted that God is incorporeal (II,9). Victor will not be able to make any progress as a theologian, in Augustine's estimation, unless he can refine his thinking
from the crude identification of corporeal with real or true to the
acknowledgement of spiritual realities and of the complexity of human knowing.

This chapter has identified the assumptions that Augustine carried with him as he entered into debate with Victor. Some had a
long pre-Christian history and their wording had become a literary
commonplace before Augustine's time. TeSelle's comment, quoted
in Chapter 1, p. 24, is appropriate here as well:

Augustine's intellectual furniture at the time of his conversion [at age 32] . . . was that of classical philosophy. He
knew nothing of Christian theology except the little he
might have gleaned from Ambrose's sermons. He was just
as much at the "beginnings" of theological reflection as, say,
Justin Martyr or Clement of Alexandria long before him.
/39/

His encounter with the Biblical tradition about knowledge apparently reinforced the classical legacy in some ways: the recognition of human limits and the dangers of transgressing them, the Socratic passion for seeking knowledge through discourse, the conviction that a human teacher is only a mediator of knowledge, not its source, the preference for human life as the material for investigation, the Socratic phrases about knowledge and ignorance together with the avowal of one's own ignorance. Both Augustine's own passage to conversion by way of an academic career and his enthusiasm for the Neoplatonist antidote to Manichaean crudity inclined him to look on classical philosophy as an ally rather than as an enemy. The one fault he found with "the Platonists" was pride. (One cannot call their incompleteness a fault since they share that with the Old Testament writers by chronological accident.) Here a new element really had entered, the humility of God Himself, which turned human judgments about knowledge and ignorance upside down. If the appeal to written authority was also a new element, Augustine was not disposed to see it as conflicting with truth arrived at through unassisted reason but rather as supplying truths otherwise inaccessible.

NOTES

/1/   The phrase "knowing what you do not know" is one translation of *scire quod nescis*, a phrase which means "to know what it is that you do not know" or "to recognize your own ignorance." I have preferred to leave it in the somewhat paradoxical-sounding form of my title since the former translation is cumbersome and the latter departs from the Latin's simple negation of the same root. The juxtaposition of opposites is a common feature of Augustine's style which I wish to preserve.

/2/   See Introduction, p. 3.

/3/   In *De Ordine* II,18,47 (PL 32, FOC 2), Augustine's definition of philosophy assumes that it is the natural activity of a Christian and that its goal is knowledge: "The study of philosophy . . . treats of two problems: one regarding the soul, and the other regarding God. The goal of the first is to know ourselves; the goal of the second is to know our origin. . . . The first is for those beginning to learn, and the other for those who are well-instructed." In the terms of this definition, Augustine's criticism of Victor would be that he has moved on to the second task without sufficient instruction. See for example I,9; II,11; II,17, where Augustine characterizes Victor as a man who has gotten in over his head.

96   Eloquence and Ignorance

/4/   Marrou makes the point strongly in *St. Augustin et la fin* . . . : "La culture intellectuelle d'Augustin est toute entière de la langue Latin," p. 37. The most exhaustive study of Augustine's knowledge of Greek is found in Pierre Courcelle's *Late Latin Writers and Their Greek Sources* (Cambridge: Harvard University Press, 1969), pp. 149–165. The consensus is that Augustine read Greek with difficulty and relied on Latin translations, although late in life he revived his Greek for the purpose of reading the Greek fathers. See, for example, Somers' article, "Image de Dieu. Les sources de l'exégèse augustinienne." REA 7 (1961), pp. 105–125. A thorough documentation of Augustine's Latin classical sources is found in Hagendahl.

/5/   Robert O'Connell, *St. Augustine's Early Theory of Man*, offers convincing proof for the long-held general opinion that the *libri platonici* are the *Enneads* of Plotinus in their Latin translation by Marius Victorinus, an older contemporary of Augustine.

/6/   Hagendahl, p. 572. TeSelle, pp. 252–255, argues that Augustine ignores some passages of the *Tim.* which would have helped his case far more than the ones he actually uses. Those he does use are the most common ones and may have come from doxographies or from Porphyry.

/7/   p. 569.

/8/   *Acad. Post.* I,4,16.

/9/   In *Eth*. VI,13 Aristotle explains that Socrates is trying to show that the separate virtues are forms of knowledge and that men only go wrong through ignorance. Aristotle disagrees with the latter view at VII,2.

/10/   OT references, Job 32:8 and 33:3. Augustine's play on the word *spiritus*, Holy Spirit and human breath, illustrates exactly the point he is trying to make to Victor: *spiritus* has numerous meanings in Scripture as in everyday speech, and one simply cannot defend a particular theory of the soul by extending the meaning that *spiritus* has in one or two passages to all of Scripture.

/11/   Quod supra nos nihil ad nos. ἃ ὑπὲρ ἡμᾶς οὐδὲν πρὸς ἡμᾶς. The saying is ascribed to Socrates by various Christian fathers (see A. Otto, *Die Sprichwörte der Römer* [Leipzig, 1890], entry No. 1714) and indeed fits very well with his portrait in Xenophon's *Mem.* I,1,11–15 and IV,7,3–8, where Socrates depreciates the study of geometry and higher mathematics on the grounds that they are not likely to be useful. Contrast this with the proposals Plato's Socrates makes in *Rep.* VII,525 ff. for the education of the guardians.

/12/   *Ep.* 166 to Jerome asking for his help on this question dates from 415. We find the problem stated much earlier also in *De Libero Arbitrio* I,2,4 (PL 32, ACW 22) (388–395): "The difficulty is: If sins go back to souls created by God and souls go back to God, how can we avoid before long tracing sin back to God?" (ACW trans.)

/13/   Sir. 3:21–22, quoted IV,5 and alluded to in chs. 6,7,8,14. My trans.

/14/   Quod supra nos, quid ad nos, above p. 85, ἅ ὑπὲρ ἡμᾶς οὐδὲν πρὸς ἡμᾶς.

/15/   *Tim.* 28c, quoted also in Justin *Apol.* II,10; Origen *Con. Cels.* VII,42; Greg. Naz. *2nd Theol. Or.* 28,4. (Trans. Jowett)

/16/   CD VIII,6.

/17/   Wisdom 13:9, RSV trans., quoted IV,6. Admittedly the Book of Wisdom does not represent pure Hebrew thought since it was written, according to scholarly opinion, at Alexandria by a Hellenized Jew in the latter part of the first century B.C. Therefore it is perhaps not a fair illustration of Hebrew as over against Greek ideas and may, insofar as it reproduces the "argument from design," reflect more a Greek than a Hebrew point of view. Armstrong and Markus observe that the Greeks saw the strongest evidence of God's presence in the constancy of cosmic processes while the Hebrews tended to see God's action demonstrated primarily in the extraordinary events, and interruptions of the usual design.

/18/   II Macc. 7:22–23. Quoted in DNOA I,23 and 25, my trans.

/19/   Augustine was always quick to appreciate the wisdom of the untutored mind, having his mother always ready to hand as an example of the knowledge that leads to salvation in contrast to the often arrogant knowledge possessed by the well-educated. His approval of the Maccabean mother reminds one of his deference to Monica in *De Beata Vita*.

/20/   I Cor. 1:25, RSV, quoted in DDC I,11. The early books of the treatise were begun in 396. I considered this passage in chapter 1 in relation to the Christian attitude toward rhetoric and philosophy, see p. 23.

/21/   DDC I,13.

/22/   See above, this ch., p. 86. Also ch. 4, p. 108.

/23/   The paradox is stated strongly by Paul in I Cor. 1:18–28; 3:18–19; 4:10; so it is not surprising that it should be important also in the fathers, especially since they are commonly learned men in the position of trying to defend the intellectual respectability of believing in revelation.

/24/   Mt. 11:25.

/25/   I Cor. 8:1.

/26/   See Introduction, p. 5.

/27/   In Book I,27 (PL 44, PNF 1st ser., 5). The full title is *De Gratia Christi et de Peccato Originali contra Pelagium.*

/28/   He goes even farther and asserts that the one who lives by faith, hope, and love can live without Scripture except as he needs it to instruct others! (Trans. LLA)

/29/   p. 433. Van der Meer also has an interesting couple of pages on the peculiar mixture in Augustine's sermons of Hellenistic intellectualism and Christian piety, pp. 448–449.

/30/   p. 539.

/31/   See Appendix B for the relevant sections of text.

/32/   This is another of those texts which expose the paradoxical character of God's dealings with man. Strength and weakness are reversed just as in the examples shown above, p. 88, where wisdom and folly trade places because of God's action.

/33/   *De Vera Religione* 24,45 (PL 34. Written 389–391), trans. G.R. Sheahan, *De vera religione* (Chapters 18–38), Master's thesis, St. Louis University, 1946, p. 27.

/34/   See the table on p. 71 of Chapter 2 above.

/35/   *Enchiridion* 17 (PL 40. Written 421–423), trans. L. A. Arand, ACW 3. The distinction between ignorance and ignorance of one's own ignorance is hardly a new one, see Plato's *Laws* IX,863c.

/36/   *Meno* 97d–99a, *Symp.* 202a, cf. *Conf.* VI,7. Nash sums it up in this way: "All learning depends on faith. If we refused to believe things we have not experienced personally, we could never know the facts of history, which are based upon the testimony of others whom we take to be authorities" (p. 25). Faith he calls "mediated scientia," "knowledge accepted on the authority of witnesses who are trustworthy" (p. 27). See all of Nash's chapter 3, "The Role of Faith."

/37/   *Retr.* I,3. See Marrou, *St. Augustin et la fin* . . . , pp. 297–308.

/38/   The passage is heavily ironic: "Nevertheless, even such a well-educated and eloquent man as you are showed your real ignorance when you believed and said and wrote and read in an assembly of invited guests that we blow up a balloon from our own nature and yet suffer no diminution of our nature. All the while, you could very easily understand how we do this, if you wanted to, not by ransacking divine and human literature but simply by observing yourself."

/39/   TeSelle, p. 55.

CHAPTER 4

SELF-KNOWLEDGE IN
DE NATURA ET ORIGINE ANIMAE

In Book II Augustine asked Peter what he had learned that he did not know before; the question was about knowing propositions, about knowledge and faith. In Book IV the central question is self-knowledge. Of all the things one could be ignorant of, the least likely is oneself. That was Victor's view. But apparently he touched a nerve, for against this particular piece of "pretending to know what one does not know," Augustine unleashed almost a whole book. If we were to give Book IV a title having to do with knowledge, it would be the ancient Delphic word: "Know thyself." We might also inscribe over it the verse of Scripture with which Victor goaded Augustine to such a long discourse on self-knowledge: "Although man was held in honor, he did not understand; he is like the cattle and can be compared to them."/1/ Augustine's references to this verse throughout DNOA, besides Book IV where he really works it through, show that he was deeply offended at being compared to a beast of the field.

Victor's accusation is the longest connected passage that Augustine quotes, and its translation is as follows:

> I know many men, doubtless experts, who have kept silence when consulted on this matter or refused to say anything very plainly; but when they undertook their exposition, they withheld any definite conclusion from their discussions. (For example: at your place recently I read and reread the contents of some writings of Augustine, a most learned man, preacher, and bishop.) In my opinion they are too modest and diffident when, after examining the mysteries of this question, they have swallowed up the conclusion of their own investigation and profess to be unable to determine anything from it. But believe me, it seems to me completely absurd and unreasonable that a human being

should lie outside his own knowledge or that one who is
supposed to have attained a conception of all things should
be thought a stranger to his own self. How then does a man
differ from a beast if he does not know how to investigate
or discuss his own quality and nature? The Scripture then
justly applies to him: "Although man was held in honor, he
did not understand; he is like the cattle and can be compared to them." For when the good God created everything
in accordance with reason, when He made man himself a
rational animal capable of understanding, endowed with
reason and alive with sensation, so that he might order all
things which lack reason by his wise arrangement, what
more incongruous thing could one say than that God with-
held from him only one sort of knowledge: that of himself.
Even the wisdom of the world strives toward knowledge of
the truth, although its investigation may be fruitless since
it cannot know the One through whom truth is known. It
has tried, nevertheless, to discern something close to the
truth, even akin to it, concerning the nature of the soul.
How unfitting and disgraceful, therefore, that any man of
religious principle should either know nothing about this
very subject or entirely forbid himself to know anything.
(IV, 2)

Like Augustine, Victor accepts the view that there are truths
about God that can be known only through revelation and are inaccessible to unassisted human reason. But Victor thinks that reason
without revelation has come pretty far regarding the problem of the
soul, too far for theologians to be justified in simply dropping the
question without applying the assistance offered by Scripture. Even
Tertullian, Victor's model in many of his ideas and someone not
noted for sympathy toward Greek philosophy, had written that the
soul's untutored witness to itself, its origin and nature, would not
conflict with the conclusions of the philosophers. That belief was
the thesis of his *De Testimonio Animae*, which Victor may well have
known.

Augustine perhaps exaggerates Victor's criticism; it likened the
man to an animal who "does not know how to investigate or discuss
his own quality and nature." Victor did not say that a man must
necessarily find the answers to these questions in order to raise
himself above brute level. It seems to a modern student ludicrous
that anyone could dare to criticize the author of the *Confessions* for
lack of introspection! There had in fact been public disapproval of
Augustine for revealing himself too plainly; no author had ever
undertaken such an unsparing exercise in self-knowledge, and the

book shocked some readers./2/ More recently *De Trinitate* had occupied him for 16 years, a work which chooses the human psyche as a source of analogies by which one may comprehend God's unity of three persons. One wonders, then, why Augustine did not meet Victor's standards of human superiority to animals since surely his writings on the soul demonstrated his ability to "investigate and discuss." But whatever Augustine did was not sufficient to satisfy Victor.

Possibly the young debater had not read any more of his opponent's work than the "litteras" (IV,2) he had found at Peter's house in Mauretania./3/ If Victor had never seen any other writings of the Bishop of Hippo, we can perhaps excuse his assumption that Augustine had given up too easily. Epistle 190 only refers in passing to "numerous works," and in fact Augustine seems to indicate that Optatus will be unacquainted with his other writings. All that the Bishop claims to give his correspondent are the chief Scriptural deterrents to taking an inflexible view, passages "which may serve to ward off temerity if not to remove doubt" (I,2).

Self-knowledge was of enormous importance to Augustine for two reasons: it was the primary clue to the knowledge of God and it was the way to happiness. The value he placed on "investigating and discussing one's own quality and nature" was probably higher than that which even Victor assigned to it. And so he finds it worthwhile to devote more space to this criticism than to the doctrinal problems Victor raises and to make a main point out of what Victor probably intended as merely an introductory blast before getting down to business.

The *beata vita* cannot be obtained without knowledge of one's true self, and that true self is the soul. The theme is not new, and it is one which cuts across the divisions between philosophical schools. The *Alcibiades* (whether it is a genuine work of Plato or not) presents the theme most explicitly in the Platonic school, while Marcus Aurelius' *Meditations* show its centrality in Stoic thought as well. It is found among ordinary folk to judge from epitaphs./4/ And Augustine is not the last to employ it either; when Boethius is languishing in prison, Philosophy tells him the reason for his unhappiness: he has forgotten who he is. That theme is also a strong one in Augustine's early works including the *Confessions*, where Augustine has not yet broken with a Neoplatonic conception of the soul as somehow burdened with a body and striving to return to its homeland./5/ Although his increasingly Biblical understanding of man as an incarnate being who will be raised bodily prevented him from viewing the body as an evil (or as a punishment, Origen's opinion, which was officially condemned by the Church in 400), nevertheless he never abandoned classical philosophy's identification of the soul with the real self.

Knowledge of self as a way to God and as a way to happiness is one single task, not two. From one of his earliest works, the *Soliloquies*, comes his famous prayer, "Deus semper idem, noverim me, noverim te" (II,1,1). A few lines later he says, "even now it is by reason of my ignorance of things and for no other reason that I am unhappy." From the same period, the discussion recorded in *De Beata Vita* leads to the conclusion that "whoever possesses God is happy" (II,12), and truth and wisdom are identified with the Son of God who is God (IV,34). Augustine could hardly have disagreed with Victor over the importance of knowing oneself, and perhaps his vehemence is a sort of exasperation at having to defend himself against one who on this point could have been an ally.

The status of the Pelagian controversy could have been another stimulus to Augustine's strong reaction against Victor's criticism. Victor and Peter were not Pelagians—Augustine shows some uncertainty about whether they will even have heard of the heresy (II,17; III,19)—but they showed the same tendency to reject the universality of sin. Pelagius and Caelestius had already been condemned by this time, in 416, but the debate with their brilliant successor, Julian of Eclanum, still lay a decade ahead, showing that the heresy was still vigorous.

To put the controversy in terms of self-knowledge, the Pelagians were fatally deluded in thinking that it lay within human power to lead a thoroughly righteous life. Augustine's own experience had brought him to know himself as proud,/6/ ruled by habit,/7/ dragged down by the deadweight of the flesh,/8/ and torn apart by conflicting wills within him./9/ The Pelagians saw no such radical problem in human nature; Pelagius accused the Catholics of slighting God's own knowledge: "We [Catholics] accuse God of a twofold ignorance,—that He does not seem to know what He has made, nor what He has commanded,—as if forgetting the human weakness of which He is Himself the Author, He has imposed laws on man which he cannot endure."/10/ One practical result of this differing concept of sin was a different understanding of baptism, and Victor had come up with the same idea as Pelagius that unbaptized infants could be saved. Victor does not seem to have reasoned out that conclusion from a Pelagian anthropology but simply to have wished to avoid the grim notion that infants are condemned for an inherited guilt. But Augustine is concerned to warn him off Pelagianism beforehand in case it should look attractive.

For these reasons, then, Augustine seized on Victor's taunt that self-knowledge easily lay within any man's grasp and heaped up evidence from medicine, everyday experience, and Biblical example to show that Victor was wrong.

In one sense the medical knowledge that Augustine drags in (IV,3; 6–7) is a red herring. Victor could not have been so dense as to imply that we must know all about the working of our bodies. There may be an element of pride in Augustine's eagerness to show off to another scholar his ready acquaintance with the various medical theories of the day./11/ He obviously finds them interesting. Most intriguing to him is the puzzling fact that the soul, in spite of its position inside the body where it ought to have access to all the body's inner workings, has to depend on the physical senses for its information. It animates the body (by definition, *anima*), but it must acquire its information about the structure and actions of the body through the physical observations made by experts (e.g., anatomists)./12/ Augustine makes no distinction here between involuntary actions the body performs, such as the beating of the heart or the growing of fingernails, and voluntary ones, such as moving a finger. The *anima* is somehow responsible for both but powerless to understand either except by observation through the senses of sight and touch.

A problem which will probably occur to a modern reader is the imprecision (to our way of thinking) of the word *anima*. The modern-day argument over whether there is such a thing as the soul is simply a linguistic impossibility in classical literature; anything that is alive, i.e., *animate*, has by definition got an *anima*. Conversely the only thing that a corpse lacks is an *anima*.

DNOA, however, is a good example of all the other ideas, both Christian and pagan, that attach to the term. To begin at the Beginning, the Genesis account says (in 2:7) that God breathed into man's nostrils and he became a living soul (*animam vivam*, IV,3). Then there is the question of how human breath (*flatus*) relates to the soul (IV,4): is it a property of the soul or of the body or of the surrounding air?/13/ When does the embryo in the womb receive its *anima* (IV,5)?/14/ When Augustine begins to speak of the "soul knowing itself" (IV,6), he has plainly added something besides mere life to the term, for it is an entity that knows, wills, and remembers (IV,9). Its modes of knowing can be distinguished (IV,31) depending on whether the senses are employed or not and what the objects to be known are. In IV,14, the soul is characterized theologically as born again, renewed, destined for eternal blessedness. The soul undergoes a preliminary judgment upon leaving the body at death and is reunited with its body at the last judgment (II,8). Are the terms "soul" (*anima*) and "inner man" (*homo interior*) interchangeable (IV,20)? What about "soul" and "spirit" (*spiritus*) (IV,36)? The soul contains images of things remembered and conceived of (IV,25), and can experience real conflict and pain in dreams (IV,26–27). But the soul does not actually leave the body when it has these dreams; otherwise the person would be dead (IV,27). The soul is awake while the body sleeps (IV,34).

This collection of references explains why the reader may feel the ground suddenly shift beneath him as he attempts to follow the arguments. Obviously to discuss "the nature of the soul" means one thing if you are talking about what differentiates a person from a corpse and quite another if you are depicting eternal blessedness. But the disputants appear not to notice any inconsistency though one wonders if the inconclusiveness of the debate might not have been mitigated by setting some limitations. However, these two men are not to blame for the confusion, nor are the Biblical writers and their interpreters. One has this same feeling of shifting sands in reading, for example, the arguments for the immortality of the soul in the *Phaedo*. Genesis and St. Paul have only complicated matters further. Because Augustine has inherited from *both* his classical and his Biblical training such a broad range of meanings for *anima*, along with the habit of slipping from one to the other, he seems not to notice the shifts. In discussing Augustine's notions of self-knowledge, i.e., of knowing one's own soul, I will try to keep clear what Augustine means by "soul" in each instance.

Since self-knowledge in both classical and Christian authors is understood as involving the "true self," the soul, Augustine's display of medical information seems, as was mentioned above (p. 105), a somewhat gratuitous addition. Yet the parts of Book IV not concerned with self-knowledge are directed against Victor's (and Tertullian's) claim that the soul is corporeal. Therefore it is not inappropriate for Augustine to bring up what pertains to the body since Victor has not defined what he means by *corpus* (IV,17). For if, as Victor maintains, the soul is a *corpus* (the same word that denotes the physical body), then distinctions in kinds of self-knowledge are broken down. Augustine's demand that Victor should prove his total understanding of his whole body and soul (since both are his own *corpora*) is a *reductio ad absurdum* of Victor's demand on Augustine that he must know where his soul came from. Thus Augustine is neatly proving two things to Victor:

1) that self-knowledge is not so simple that one should mock confessed ignorance, and
2) that calling the soul *corpus* and putting it into the same category as the physical body results in patently absurd demands on self-understanding.

By dealing first with the body, Augustine exposes the folly of believing that self-knowledge will be easy. The soul must be "higher" than the body, in a sense, since without it the body cannot act. If we know so little about even this "lower" element of our being, why should we think it will be easy to know about the higher part?

Time works against us too. If we know so little about what is at this present moment going on inside of us, how will we easily know what happened at or before our birth?

> My soul is not at this moment being derived from my parents or being breathed into me by God; whichever of these two He did, He did at the time He created me and He is not doing it now for me or in me. That deed is over and done with; it is neither present to me now nor is it recent. Nor do I even know whether I knew it and have forgotten or whether I was incapable even at the time the deed was done of perceiving or knowing it. (IV,8)

Even infancy is beyond our memory and we are dependent for knowledge about our birth and first years on the word of others (IV,5–6).

However, Augustine carefully avoids an equation of what is high with what is difficult to know. We do know something about God, after all, even though a far more mundane question like, How many animals entered Noah's ark? is beyond us (IV,6). Nevertheless Scripture warns against seeking out what is too high for human understanding (Sir. 3:21). The origin of the soul may well be such a question.

This might look as if Augustine were ducking out of the argument, simply removing it from the agenda. But then why does Book IV go on for 34 chapters wrestling with the same question? I have mentioned that the search for self-knowledge was an important, rather, a necessary exercise for the Christian, in Augustine's view, and the author of the *Confessions* has no rival in pressing to the limit the insoluble questions of his existence. Such a mind is not likely to draw back out of timidity. Dogmatic considerations are part of the reason for Augustine's hesitation,/15/ but the impulse to silence before the mysteries of God is not a Christian innovation raised by the appearance of religious dogma. The Old Testament writers who pleaded with God, challenged Him, quarreled with Him, bargained with Him, prevailed on Him to change His mind, and attributed to Him many of their own less admirable emotions, nevertheless stopped dead in their tracks when struck by the sense of awe. Job finally lays his hand upon his mouth and repents his questioning in dust and ashes./16/ The Psalmist hears "Be still and know that I am God."/17/

Augustine's hesitation has in it not only his Biblical inheritance but a reminiscence of Greek piety much older than Neoplatonism, than Plato even. γνῶθι σεαυτόν was not originally the philosophical call to look at one's own soul but a caution against misjudging one's place in the universe. Its position at Delphi with μηδὲν ἄγαν reminded man that he was not God. Greek tragedy presents one man whose self-knowledge is complete—and that is Oedipus. Even his name is a pun on knowledge. He knows that *man* is the answer to the riddle of the Sphinx; he learns his own origins. But the cost to him is beyond comprehension. Mythology shows the tragedy of Narcissus, warned before his fatal obsession with self-knowledge, that he will live only as long as he does not know himself. Augustine's vision, though it has a warning tone, is less terrifying than the tragedians', even considering his picture of the Christians' God who judges. For this God also chooses to reveal Himself and may yet (through Scripture or reason) make known to us the origin of the soul (IV,5). Victor's spirit ought to be one of patience before the knowledge that is "too wonderful" for him (Ps. 138/139:6, quoted IV,12).

Augustine never uses the proverb γνῶθι σεαθτόν in this treatise although it appears in some of his other writings./18/ Where he does use it, it is always in the later sense of entering into one's soul to seek wisdom and to find God, not in the archaic sense of avoiding hubris. His admonitions not to overstep the assigned limits of human knowledge have a Biblical rather than a classical reference in DNOA. But the warning could have been sounded as well from classical as from Biblical antecedents: the defense of Christian dogma was *one* of Augustine's motives for argument but not the only one. One notes that while Augustine's arguments are taken from Scripture, the whole discussion revolves around Greek formulae: "knowing what you do not know" and "know thyself." The consequences of pride are an ancient theme, not only signs of a new authoritarianism.

With a fine rhetorical passage on the mystery of ourselves, /19/ Augustine introduces three figures who illustrate the paucity of our self-knowledge in respect to memory, understanding, and will; they are respectively Simplicius, Paul, and Peter. The meditative passage of IV,9 is an echo of *De Trinitate* X,11,17, written a few years earlier:

> Ecce modo, modo dum sumus, dum vivimus, dum nos vivere scimus, dum meminisse nos et intellegere et velle certissimi sumus, qui nos naturae nostrae magnos cognitores esse iactamus, quid valeat memoria nostra vel intelligentia vel voluntas omnino nescimus. (DNOA IV,9)

> Remotis igitur paulisper ceteris, quorum mens de se ipsa certa est, tria haec potissimum considerata tractemus, memoriam, intelligentiam, voluntatem. (*De Trin.*X,11,17)

Note that there are things the mind is sure of, but the question is *quid valent?* We do not know.

Simplicius, who finds that he knows both Vergil and Cicero quite literally backwards and forwards, is astonished at his own power of memory (IV,9). He only came to know himself capable of such an extraordinary feat when asked. Augustine modestly shows himself as an illustration of the opposite and far more common sort of ignorance, failure of memory, or more accurately the seemingly independent character of memory (IV,10). The musings on memory and forgetting show a peculiar conception of the process./20/ Instead of implying that the objects of memory reside, so to speak, in the mind and can somehow escape or become lost from it, Augustine's description implies it is the *self* that departs, as though the contents of memory were the basic reality and the self periodically lost its bearings and wandered off. The picture seems quite the opposite of what we would assume, and a disconcerting picture at that. As the writer says (IV,10), "Nonne adtendis et exhorrescis tantam profunditatem?" Forgetfulness of this kind is far more serious than a temporary loss of a small piece of one's property. It is the threat of losing one's identity. Augustine says of Simplicius that he was obviously the same man before and after his astonishing discovery (IV,9), but immediately (IV,10) he falls into the other imagery with a series of questions, some unanswered:

> Does that mean we were not ourselves when we were thinking of [a particular bit of knowledge]? Nevertheless, we are not what we were when we were unable to think of it. How is it then that in some way we are abstracted from and denied to ourselves and subsequently restored somehow and given back to ourselves? It is as though we were different people or in some other place when we seek but do not find what we have stored in our memory; and we are unable to return to ourselves, as though we were in another place, and then we return to ourselves when we have found it. For where should we seek other than within ourselves? Or what should we seek if not ourselves (as if we were not in ourselves and had departed from ourselves to some other place)?

The paradox is, I think, a variation on the immanence/transcendence theme from the *Confessions*, still unresolved after 20 years. In Book X (which Ryan's translation entitles "A Philosophy of Memory") one finds the same shifting reflection between God within and God without, between a soul traveling inward and outward (I have italicized some phrases to illustrate the opposing ideas):

> . . . but you remain unchangeable *above* all things. And you have deigned to dwell *in my memory*, whence I have learned of you. . . . Truly, you dwell *in my memory* . . . and I find you there when I call you to mind. . . . Where then did I find you, so that I might learn to know you? You were *not in my memory* before I learned to know you. Where then have I found you, if not *in yourself and above me*? There is *no place*, both backward do we go and forward. . . . *Everywhere*, O Truth. . . . You were *within* me, while *I was outside*. . . . You were with me, but I was not with you. (*Conf.* X, chs. 25–27)

O'Connell /21/ attributes the audacious combination of metaphors to the dual heritage of Augustine's conversion years, the Christian theology of omnipresence mingling with the emanationist scheme of the *Enneads*. Even Plotinus's soul both strives toward the One Beyond Being and yet is itself divine. The soul in DNOA which holds memory and understanding intact is the real self bearing God's image (IV,20). Forgetting and ignorance are then a decline

from the real self and from God—in a sense, the loss of one's true
identity and a change into some other inauthentic self./22/

There is, however, a Scriptural "forgetting" that is not a decline
but is actually enjoined on us by Paul: "Forgetting those things
which are behind, straining forward to those things which are
ahead, I press on toward the goal. . . . "/23/ For Augustine the text
seems especially appropriate to the present debate since we have
indeed forgotten our infancy and the soul's origin but have before
us the promise of the soul's destiny to eternal life (IV,14).

Our understanding shows the same perverse tendency as memory to fail us when we are confronted with a question and to reap-
pear when we have ceased to look for the answer. We have come
back to the "knowing what you do not know" theme. Surely Victor
has *something* which he wishes to understand. His very desire to
understand presumes a hope for success. Why not admit this common ignorance, this weakness in which strength is perfected?/24/

Augustine adds some Biblical examples to his personal one:
Paul's mysterious reference to being caught up into the third
heaven,/25/ his conviction of the Spirit's assistance to our prayers,
/26/ and his actual praying of the wrong prayer that proved his ignorance./27/ The third-heaven experience is the subject of the entire Book XII of *De Genesi ad Litteram*. There Augustine asked,
"How can he be certain about what he saw and uncertain about the
manner in which he saw it?" The question and analysis of Paul's
vision lead Augustine to a discussion of the three levels of vision
which he names corporeal, spiritual (resembling most what we
would call the power of imagination), and intellectual./28/ Paul's experience is another instance of Augustine's observation that the
things too high for us are not necessarily heavenly things: Paul knew
magna, alta atque divina (IV,12) of the heavenly realm but could
not tell about his own self whether he was in the body or not.

Equally surprising to Augustine is the apostle's ignorance which
he avowed in saying "We do not know how to pray as we ought"
(Rom. 8:26, RSV). Augustine wants Victor to note the humility of
"the great teacher of the Gentiles," (IV,13), who admitted his ignorance and then proceeded to prove it by praying for the removal of
his "thorn in the flesh" (II Cor. 12:7–8). God's refusal showed that
Paul had indeed been ignorant of how he ought to pray.

The apostle Peter, Augustine's third and final example, illustrates a remarkable contrast between knowledge of a high order and

ignorance of one's own power of will (IV,11). He shows divinely-inspired knowledge in confessing that Jesus is the Son of God. Later, in ignorance of his own weakness, he promises to die for his Lord and instead denies him. Augustine has chosen his examples carefully. If Victor is going to compare to cattle anyone who does not know his own self completely, he will have to include not only Augustine but the two greatest saints and champions of the Church.

Why did Victor choose the "cattle" text and what does Augustine do with it? The Bishop suspects that Victor has picked that particular verse because of the reference to honor, meaning Augustine's exalted position in the Church (IV,3), "unlike yourself." He does not, however think it is at all relevant to Victor's topic but rather concerns those who "regard this life as the only one, living according to the flesh and hoping for nothing after death, like cattle" (IV,15)./29/ He presses Victor ironically to be more precise (IV,3):

> I would like to know how much and to what degree you
> would concede [that there are things pertaining to our own
> nature which we do not know]. . . . Perhaps you think that
> one is allowed only as much ignorance of his own nature as
> you have and as much knowledge of it as you have been
> able to acquire. Hence, if anyone is a little more ignorant
> than you are, you may compare him to cattle because you
> have been able to acquire more knowledge than he,
> whereas if anyone knows a little more than you, he may
> with equal justice compare you to cattle. Well, tell us then
> to what extent you permit us to be ignorant of our own
> nature so that we may keep a safe distance from the cattle.

He concludes with a Socratic twist:

> Think it over carefully, lest he who knows that he is some-
> what ignorant of this [subject] be further from the cattle
> than he who thinks he knows what he does not know.

Augustine rebukes his impatience with those who do not know all about such matters; after all, the medical people do not call *us* cattle just because we are ignorant of their subject. He gets carried away into boasting but then tries to soften the effect:

> I would fill up many volumes if I wanted to show how much
> I can discuss intelligently about the nature of man;/30/
> nevertheless I confess that there is much I do not know.
> (IV,3).

When the verse comes up again in IV,14, Augustine tries to pin Victor down for inconsistency. If knowing how to discuss and investigate the nature of the soul is something only revelation imparts, then no credit attaches to the man who can fulfill it; it is God's gift. If it is a natural attribute that needs no divine help, why does Victor drag in all those Scriptural texts, as though only a person who can read is superior to cattle? The last supposition Augustine finds ridiculous. Human beings *are* better than animals but not because they can read. Actually all the protestations about our ignorance of self are for the sake of argument. Augustine knows perfectly well that we do know ourselves better than anyone else because "we know our own consciousness and disposition" (IV,30). But if knowledge were really only connected to *bodies*, as Victor implies, we would have to take frequent looks in the mirror to keep from forgetting ourselves (IV,21)./31/ Even so, our mirror image would only be a superficial sort of knowledge of the outer person. There truly is such a thing as the inner man for Augustine but the reason we know him well is not, as Victor theorized, because he looks like a slightly smaller version of the outer man but because we have the faculty of knowing things other than corporeal objects or likenesses of them (IV,31)./32/ As the soul is higher than the body, so the faculty of the soul by which we know incorporeal realities (faith, hope, love, God) is higher than the five senses (which enable us to know corporeal things) and the imagination (which holds likenesses of corporeal things).

IV,31 says that in this highest faculty of the soul "we are to be renewed in the knowledge of God after the image of Him who created us." In this belief Augustine follows in a line from Origen, who placed God's image in man's soul, more particularly in his mind./33/ This interpretation had enabled Ambrose to refute the Manichaean taunt that Christians worshipped a god with fingernails and hair, /34/ and it was natural that Augustine should follow his mentor against the heresy which had so long plagued him. It is somewhat inconsistent, then, that Augustine mocks Victor's Chinese-box anthropology, spirit-inside-a-soul-inside-a-body, by asking him which part it is that will receive God's image.

> Does [the inner man] have two images, God's from above
> and the body's from below like what we call heads and tails
> on a coin [literally "head and ship"]? (IV,20)

Augustine must, like Victor, be thinking of a physical image. Likewise when he asks how, if the soul is a body, it could receive the image of a God who is not a body, Augustine seems to be putting the *imago Dei* in physical terms, although that may be a deliberate step—adopting Victor's materialist assumptions in order to demolish them.

One notes in the quotation at the beginning of the preceding paragraph the necessity for renewal. The image of God is indisputably there, but it has been damaged by the Fall. The presence of sin is what makes the quest for self-knowledge so arduous and dependent upon divine assistance. Victor seems not to have taken that into account although there is that one curious phrase which one wishes might have been given in context:

> If the soul, which could not be sinner, deserved to be a sinner, it still did not remain in sin since it was *prefigured in Christ* that it must not be in sin, just as it could not be. (I,8, see above ch. 2, p. 59)

Does "prefigured in Christ" indicate some idea of renewal of the soul through its identification with Christ's death and resurrection? There is too little of the context to tell what Victor had in mind, and Augustine does not pick up on the phrase.

Regardless of how one understands it, the Genesis assertion that God created man in His own image forms the bridge which, for Christian writers, connects knowledge of oneself with the knowledge of God. It was this link to which Victor appealed in his opening question directed at Augustine:

> When the good God created everything in accordance with reason, when He made man himself a rational animal capable of understanding, . . . what more incongruous thing could one say than that God withheld from him only one sort of knowledge, that of himself? (IV,2)

Though adversaries on particular points,/35/ Augustine and Victor share this faith, not just as Christians but as heirs of classical philosophy, that the world is intelligible. Both are sure, in spite of their disagreements, that the clues to the structure of reality lie within the mind.

I have devoted two chapters to analyzing what Augustine says about knowledge in DNOA and only one to what he says about the soul, ostensibly the subject of his book. The disproportion is, however, true to Augustine's own concerns in the treatise. Once the question about the soul has led to a dead end, Augustine is forced to defend his indecision by showing why certain knowledge is impossible. Yet the disproportion also reveals the utter consistency of Augustine's quest: that in a relatively late work the hunger for knowledge of God and of the self retains all its former urgency. The philosophic goal of his contemplative period at Cassiciacum, to know God and the soul,/36/ survives undiminished, but it has been transformed from a solitary pursuit, as in the early dialogues, into a topic for persuasion. Augustine puts all his rhetorical skill to work on Victor to turn him away from error and pride and to insure the safety of the Church from heresy. The methods of that persuasion will be the subject of the next chapter.

NOTES

/1/   Ps. 48/49:13 (LXX). The verse as it appears in the RSV (Ps. 49:12) from the Hebrew is scarcely recognizable: "Man cannot abide in his pomp, he is like the beasts that perish." It would be interesting to compile a list of texts where an auspicious mistranslation has formed the basis of an elaborate theological construct. The two that come to mind in Augustine are Is. 7:9 ("If you do not believe, you will not understand") from which comes Augustine's *credo ut intellegam* and Sirach 18:1 ("omnia *simul* creavit") which Augustine adopts as the exegetical principle for interpreting Genesis.

/2/   See chapter 7 "Jugements des contemporains" in Courcelle's *Recherches sur les 'Confessions' de St. Augustin* (Paris: E. de Boccard, 1968).

/3/   Augustine calls it "*nonnullum opusculum*" in *Retr.* II,56. De Veer in his article "Aux origines" identifies the treatise to which Victor's books are directed as Epistle 190 to Optatus on the origin of the soul. It fulfills the description which Victor gives, denying the corporeality of the soul and avowing ignorance of its origin. Chronologically it fits the course of the debate.

/4/   See Richmond Lattimore, *Themes in Greek and Latin Epitaphs* (Urbana: University of Illinois Press, 1962), pp. 49–55.

/5/   Whether Augustine believed in a preexistent soul early in his career is still debated. See R. O'Connell's "Pre-existence in Augustine's Seventh Letter," REA 15 (1969), pp. 67–73, and G. O'Daly, "Did Augustine Ever Believe in the Soul's Pre-existence?" *Augustinian Studies* 5 (1974), pp. 227–235 for pro and con arguments. In his old age he explicitly rejected the idea (*Retr.* I,8,2), but what he takes exception to in DNOA is not so much the idea of preexistence *per se* as Victor's inconsistency in implying sometimes that man deserves rewards and other times that he deserves punishment (II,11) as a result of some good or bad preexistent state. Te-Selle sees a shift in Augustine's thinking about preexistence and hereditary original sin around the year 406. He speculates that the controversy over Origen's theology about that time and his condemnation in 400 forced Augustine to rethink his views (pp. 258–264). The theme of return to one's true self, and thus to God is illustrated in *Conf.* VII,10,16: "Being thus admonished to return to myself, under your leadership, I entered into my inmost being. This I could do, for you became my helper. I entered there, and by my soul's eye . . . saw . . . an unchangeable light." Speaking of the Incarnation, "He departed from our eyes so that we might return into our own hearts and find him there" (*Conf.* IV,12,19, trans. Ryan).

/6/   e.g., *Conf.* III,5,9; V,10,18; VII,9,13.

/7/   ". . . the law of sin is force of habit, whereby the mind is dragged along and held fast, even against its will, but still deservedly so since it was by its will that it had slipped into the habit" (*Conf.* VIII,5,12, Ryan trans.).

/8/   "I was borne up to you by your beauty, but soon I was borne down from you by my own weight, and with groaning, I plunged into the midst of those lower things. This weight was carnal custom" (*Conf.* VII,17,23).

/9/   "Mind commands mind to will; there is no difference here, but it does not do so. Whence comes this monstrous state? . . . it is a sickness in the mind" (*Conf.* VIII,9,21, Ryan trans.).

/10/   *Ep. to Demetrias*, 16 (PL 30, FOC trans.).

/11/   In *Cat. Rud.* Augustine recommends meeting the educated student on his own ground as far as possible (I,8,12), and he certainly follows his own advice with regard to Victor.

/12/   Augustine mentions the dissection by the anatomists of live human bodies (IV,3). In CD XXII,24, he speaks with distaste of the surgeons who "have ruthlessly applied themselves to the carving up of dead bodies" and "have cut into the bodies of dying men to make their examinations" (Bettenson trans.). Augustine's source for Bk. IV is possibly the medical writings of a contemporary, Vindicianus, of whose work we have only fragments. (See BA 48, n. 34, "Augustin et la science médicale.") Augustine speaks of attending his lectures in *Conf.* IV,3,5.

/13/   The Stoics identified the soul with breath (*spiritus*) and therefore considered it material. By Augustine's time the mainstream of Christian thought, under the influence of Neoplatonism, regarded the soul as a spiritual, immaterial reality. See Verbeke for the history of the "spiritualization" of *pneuma*; see also above Chapter 2, pp. 44–50.

/14/   Tertullian (*De An*. 25,9) said that it entered at the moment of conception since he defined life as the union of soul and body (27,2) and obviously the child in the womb is alive (again *anima* = life). The Stoic Chrysippus thought that the ψυχή came into being at the child's birth as soon as it met the surrounding air, probably a desire to link ψυχή etymologically with ἀναψύχω (to cool off), a connection found in Plato's *Cratylus* 399e (see Verbeke, p. 80).

/15/   The theories of the origin of the soul conflicted with the doctrines of original sin and the goodness of God's creation, see Intro., pp. 7–8.

/16/   Job 40:4; 42:6.

/17/   Ps. 46:10, RSV.

/18/   The exhaustive study of the proverb is Pierre Courcelle's 3-volume work, '*Connais-toi toi-même*' *de Socrate à St. Bernard* (Paris: Études augustiniennes, 1974), to which this chapter is indebted for background material. Why Augustine does not use what would seem a most obviously appropriate commonplace is perhaps a reflection of what he knows of Victor's training. DNOA lacks classical allusions except for the medical sections, where his aim is partly to impress. He seems uninterested in bringing in proofs other than Scripture even though he was at this time working on CD, which shows evidence of wide reading in secular authors.

/19/   IV,8, quoted in chapter 5, p. 134.

/20/   See Appendix B for translation of IV,9–10 on memory.

/21/   *St. Augustine's Early Theory of Man: 386–391*.

/22/   One finds in Plato some comparable sense of memory as necessary to a good life. *Phaedr*. 250a speaks of the forgetfulness of true being, of that vision which the soul formerly had. *Rep*. VI has several references (484b, 486c, 487a, 490c) to the necessity of a good memory if one is to be a philosopher.

/23/   Phil. 3:13–14, quoted IV,12.

/24/   II Cor. 12:9.

/25/   II Cor. 12:4.

/26/   Rom. 8:26.

/27/   II Cor. 12:7–8.

/28/   *De Gen*. XII,13–16. The categories correspond precisely to those in DNOA IV,31, quoted above in ch. 3, p. 93.

/29/   In CD XXII,24, Augustine alludes to this same verse in connection with the Fall's effect on human propagation: "Comparatus est pecoribus, similiter generat"!

/30/   Courtès doubts whether that is true, "St. Augustin et la médecine," *Augustinus Magister* I (Paris, 1954), pp. 43–51.

/31/   The mirror is associated with self-knowledge in traditions about Socrates, in the Stoics, in Gnostic writers, even in the Bible (James 1:23–24). For examples see Courcelle's index under *speculum*. It is interesting that Augustine uses it in the opposite way here, not as a help to knowing oneself but as an instrument of delusion, giving one a false presumption of self-knowledge.

/32/   The passage is quoted in full in ch. 3, p. 93.

/33/   See BA 48, n. 15, "La doctrine augustinienne de l'image et la tradition patristique" and n. 16, "L'âme image de Dieu." Also H. Somers, "Image de Dieu. Les sources de l'exégèse augustinienne," REA 7 (1961), pp. 105–125.

/34/   *Conf.* III,7,12.

/35/   In Book III,3–7, Augustine argues against Victor's most serious error—that the soul is part of the substance of God. If Victor were to follow this line of reasoning, he would be in danger of understanding self-knowledge in the sense of the Stoic formulation of the "Dream of Scipio": "deum te scito." "Augustin se sépare à la fois des Stoïciens et des Néoplatoniciens selon lesquels se connaître soi-même est connaître Dieu en soi" (Courcelle,*Connais-toi . . .*, p. 144.)

/36/   *Solil.* 1,7.

CHAPTER 5

AUGUSTINE AND HIS ADVERSARY

No other work of Augustine's gives us quite the opportunity to examine in a small space his treatment of an opponent. In DNOA we have Augustine's refutation of two books by a young man whom he considers to hold a number of potentially heretical ideas; but the Bishop himself joined to his two books of rebuttal two more epistles, one to the man who had had Victor's books sent to him and one to the priest who had encouraged Victor's writing and approved of his finished work. Thus we can view this controversy from three angles, observing how the Bishop of Hippo conforms his style, his arguments, and his tone to the character of his correspondent.

Augustine's skill at observing what Aristotle defined by the terms λόγος, ἦθος, and πάθος/1/ is summarized thus by Finaert:

> Selon le public auquel il s'adresse, selon les sujets, les circonstances, les sentiments qui l'animent, il donne à sa pensée le tour qui convient./2/

Augustine's earliest rhetorical training would have taught him the formal categories of argumentation and the kinds of audiences receptive to them, but appropriateness was a subject to which he had given much subsequent thought as well. From his work as an instructor of new converts came De Catechizandis Rudibus (405), a book any teacher would find profitable for its attention to the psychology of learning. His return to the unfinished De Doctrina Christiana at the very end of his career (427) after a gap of 30 years revealed his concern for the art of Christian preaching. This chapter will look at the language Augustine uses—especially at how it conforms to the character of each recipient.

The controversy itself was a small one when compared with the struggles that occupied Augustine's term as Bishop of Hippo: first the long battle with the Donatists and later the defense against Pelagianism. Less was at stake here. The question of the origin of the soul did not involve such central elements of the Church's teaching as those two heresies, which threatened respectively the unity of the Church and the Church's understanding of grace./3/ In fact Au gustine, in this case, far from defending dogma, stoutly maintained his right to leave the question of the soul's origin open and refused to allow his opponent to push a peripheral issue into the center.

This is not to say that Augustine regarded the whole affair as unimportant. He did trouble himself to answer Renatus's letter immediately (I,35). Victor's theories about the soul brought up matters which he could not consider merely peripheral, the more dangerous because Victor did not realize their import. The inquiries of Optatus/4/ and references within DNOA/5/ indicate a whole party of questioners in Mauretania for whom the soul's nature and origin was a hot issue, and Augustine saw how dangerously ready a whole group of clergy and educated lay people might be to succumb to Pelagian ideas. Besides, Orosius had informed him that Origenist and Priscillianist views still survived in Spain,/6/ and Victor's listeners might well find these heresies attractive if prepared for them by Victor's speculations. The matter held potential trouble for Church order; yet it required pastoral persuasion rather than the severely authoritarian action which finally attended the Donatist and Pelagian affairs.

This treatise shows Augustine in correspondence with three people, but these letters are no more intended for private perusal than were, say, Pliny's. As the Bishop writes to his opponent and his acquaintances, he has in mind a far larger audience. Victor's attack on Augustine had not been merely a letter or a pamphlet but a public recitation, and Augustine is quite aware that his reply will be circulated. In fact he suggests to Renatus the circulation of the epistle (I,35), and in his letters to the other two, he urges them to contact Renatus. The letters, then, will address their recipients appropriately. But more than that, they will instruct a much wider circle—something at which the great preacher of Hippo is a master. They will beg to be read aloud./7/

The letters are self-consciously eloquent not only because of the public character of the correspondence but because their author well realizes his own position. Augustine knows perfectly well that he is the spokesman for the faith, at least in the West. (Jerome acknowledged Augustine's preeminence in Epistle 195 and at one time advised caution lest any apparent disagreement between them should encourage heretics [Epistle 172].) However, Augustine writes also with the confidence of a winner; he is conscious of a tradition behind him lending strength to the defense of orthodoxy. The Fathers of the Church recognized the appearance of heresy as a necessary evil, one prophesied in the New Testament (e.g., I Cor. 11:19; I Jn. 4:1), but destined to be unsuccessful. Augustine replies to Victor (III,1–2) not as one whose success depends on winning the argument at hand but as a champion of the truth that Victor must inevitably come to recognize.

Augustine was once criticized for not taking an opponent seriously enough (*Ep.* 148,4). There is some truth in the accusation to this extent: the conviction that Truth must win out in the end delivers the Christian apologist from any illusion that he bears the entire responsibility for the success or failure of an argument./8/ However that same conviction gives him an added earnestness in relation to the *persons* he is arguing against, for their salvation becomes his responsibility, in a sense. Augustine certainly demonstrates this seriousness in his indefatigable production of letters, sermons, and books answering the questions of both friends and adversaries. If he occasionally dismisses a proposition with some impatience or sophistry or flippancy, still he treats its defender with the gravity appropriate to a *Seelsorger.*

Our treatise illustrates this point admirably: Books I-III handle the same material, and most of the same arguments are listed and refuted. Would not a single treatise have sufficed, carbon copies to the other two men, to settle the matter? The writer does not think so and from the first (I,5; I,35) intends to write to Victor himself even though he knows that Renatus will circulate his letter and see that Victor and his partisans hear it. The letter to Renatus is really directed at Victor (witness the large number of jussives—"Let him . . . "), and he thinks of the effect it will have on the young man (I,2). But his response to Victor himself shows that he has taken some trouble to find out more about his challenger (III,2) so that he may reason with him more effectively.

Of the three recipients, Renatus is the only one whom Augustine knows personally. He figured earlier in the correspondence with Optatus over the origin of the soul./9/ Since he was a lay monk, he would probably have approached Augustine with a good deal of deference, even apprehension, in bringing a less-than-complimentary challenge to the attention of a superior. Augustine is anxious to calm his misgivings and to assure him that he has acted properly.

Indeed he rather gracefully raises the monk to the level of colleague in I,3 by approving of Renatus' assessment of Victor's style. He is genuinely appreciative of his theological concern and grateful to him for looking out for his reputation. One might dismiss Renatus' solicitude as apple-polishing were it not for the evidence of his earlier interest in the theological issue. The fact that Augustine never talks down to Renatus, either on matters of theology or style proves his respect for the monk's intelligent acquaintance with the controversy.

Books II and III single out eleven particular statements made by Victor which Augustine finds unacceptable. Though Book I covers most of these errors, they are not enumerated specifically. Instead, four errors not Victor's own but which might be implied from his statements are listed more than once. Is it for the simple practical reason that Augustine is replying in haste and has not yet had time to think over Victor's writings? Or is it that Augustine's preoccupation during this period with the Pelagians disposes him to see Pelagianism lurking behind every questionable proposition? Probably both are true, but a third reason may be that Book I is intended for the widest audience./10/ Augustine wants his first blast at Victor's circle to explode the foundations of his critic's arguments. Then in the subsequent books he can pick off the superstructure bit by bit.

Renatus was not only displeased at Victor's theology; he also disliked his writing style./11/ Augustine agrees with Renatus that Victor's eloquence is often superficial. False eloquence may be merely frivolous or it may be downright dangerous if it seduces its hearers into false doctrine./12/ But Augustine appears more ready than Renatus to make allowances for Victor's youth and to assume that good will and concern for truth underlie his attack.

Augustine's evaluation of Victor's rhetorical talents is itself a careful—and colorful—piece of rhetoric. Victor is to be gently corrected "ne faciat esse delectabilia quae sunt inutilia" (the homoioteleuton of which Augustine is so fond); even if his style should remain more florid than one would like, still "a levibus mentibus amatur, toleratur a gravibus" (an example of chiasmus followed by an alliterative phrase, "quosdam spumeos in sermone, sed in fide sanos"). Augustine never hesitates to pile up similar-ending words as in ". . . expurgari et temperari atque ad integrum et solidum vel perduci vel revocari modum," and just a couple of lines later, "illud molestum est et periculosum vel perniciosum, si, cum laudatur elo*quentia*, persuade*atur* insip*ientia*." The part of the latter example, beginning with *si* echoes the preceding "Quod minus habet peritia suppleat diligentia."/13/ Within two sentences we find two vivid metaphors related to eating and drinking, the first employing homoioteleuton and the second alliteration: "quod crud*itas* loquac*itatis* eruc*tat*, ae*tatis* matur*itas* decoqu*at*," and "in *p*retioso *p*oculo bibatur *p*estifera *p*otio."/14/

Even when Augustine enters into the argument proper, he is attentive to the sound of his sentences. For example in I,9, the rapid fire of questions builds to the climax:

> Dicat meritum eius utrum bonum fuerit anne malum. Si bonum, quo merito bono venit in malum? Si malum, unde aliquod malum meritum ante omne peccatum? Item dico: Si bonum, non ergo eam gratis, sed secundum debitum liberat gratia, cuius praecessit meritum bonum, ac sic gratia iam non erit gratia; si autem malum, quaero quod sit: an quod venit in carnem, quo non venisset nisi apud quem non est iniquitas ipse misisset?"/15/

Victor has presented two examples to support his contention that those who die unbaptized can inherit the kingdom of heaven: the repentant thief and Dinocrates, the brother of St. Perpetua. Augustine argues that the former example will hardly fit the case of infants or unbelievers since plainly faith was present and, in a sense, a martyr's death. The passage on the thief, more than any other in this treatise, represents Augustine the preacher. Beginning with a striking figure of a blossoming tree, the author builds an ascending series of rhythmically-balanced antitheses. I have written this out in such a way that the symmetry shows clearly (see pp. 124–25).

One regrets that Victor's work is no longer extant, for it would be interesting to see to what degree Augustine follows the rhetorical style of his opponent. Occasionally we *can* observe the use Augustine makes of Victor's cues. One such example is the metaphor of shipwreck in I,9, which Victor directs against Augustine and others:

> Alia substruuntur obprobria querulis murmurationibus oblatrantum et excussi quasi quodam turbine identidem inter immania saxa conlidimur.

The quotation is loaded with alliteration and assonance, and Augustine's reply picks up the style: ". . . tam horrendis cautibus inlatus, inpulsus, infixus, ut eruere se nisi emendando quod dixit omnino non possit. . . ." He has used the image of shipwreck before:

Tunc enim

fides eius de ligno floruit

quando discipulorum marcuit

nisi

cuius mortis terrore marcuerat

eius resurrectione revivesceret.

Illi enim desperaverunt de moriente,
refugerunt illi auctorem vitae
doluerunt illi tamquam hominis mortem
deseruerunt illi sponsorem salutis

ille speravit in commoriente;
rogavit ille consortem poenae;
credidit ille regnaturum esse post mortem;
honoravit ille socium crucis.

quando defecerunt
qui futuri erant martyres.

Inventa est in eo mensura martyris
qui tunc in Christum credidit
Et hoc quidem oculis Domini clarum fuit, qui
non baptizato   tamquam   martyrii sanguine abluto
tantam felicitatem statim contulit.
Sed etiam nostrum
quis non consideret

quanta fide,
quanta spe,
quanta caritate
qui vitam in moriente quaesivit?

mortem pro Christo vivente suscipere potuit

(I,11)

For

at the same time as

the disciples' faith withered

except that

at His resurrection it revived again.

For

he

hoped in the one dying with him

he

besought the sharer of his punishment

he

believed that he would rule after death

he

honored the companion of his cross.

those failed

who were to become martyrs.

his faith blossomed from the wood

in terror at whose death it withered

they

despaired regarding the one dying

they

fled from the author of life

they

grieved as though at a man's death

they

deserted the guarantor of their salvation

There was found in him the full measure of a martyr

who believed in Christ   at the time when

And this was very plain in the eyes of the Lord

who

at once conferred such happiness on one

but

as it were

But who of us could not perceive with

unbaptized

washed by martyr's blood

what hope

he

what faith

what love

could have undergone death

for a living Christ

who sought life

from a dying one.

In huius quaestionis tamquam scopuloso gurgite debuit utique cavere naufragium nec eo se committere, unde se non erueret transeundo, sed forte redeundo, id est paenitendo. (I, 7)

and returns to it in II, 18:

. . . maluit per naufragium miserabile exire quam temerarium cursum, velis depositis et remis suae disputationis inhibitis, provida deliberatione frenare.

Out of this second reference, Augustine constructs a double pun:

Cum enim nollet cohibere *praecipitem cursum* propter *ancipitem excursum*, miserabilem invenit *incursum*. . . .

If Augustine is more ready than Renatus to overlook Victor's shortcomings as a rhetorician, he is also willing to attribute his theological blunders to his youth rather than to incompetence or ill will. He excuses Victor to Renatus for writing without his knowledge on the grounds that Victor must have believed in the invincibility of his case (I, 2). Augustine does not wish Renatus to judge the young man harshly but to cooperate in the effort to persuade him gently of his error. Again Augustine acts graciously in treating Renatus as a colleague, not an inferior.

The case is rather different with Peter, to whom Book II is addressed. Renatus had been critical of Victor's work, both style and substance; Peter, on the other hand, had encouraged Victor's writing in the first place and received the finished product with open arms (literally, see II, 1). So whereas Augustine had seen fit to urge gentleness and sympathy in the monk's treatment of the young author, he wants to arouse Peter to a much more critical appraisal of Victor's work. He is much harder on Peter than either of the other two, and the reason is that Peter of all people should have known better. He is a priest and an old man, so that both training and experience should have prepared him to discriminate between legitimate expressions of faith and vaguely heretical ideas. Moreover his position of authority as priest and presbyter affects other Christians; if he is led astray, so will they be. He has apparently acted as a sort of patron to Victor and as his mentor in the faith./16/ Of what use is it, asks Augustine, if "the sheep which comes from his error into the Lord's flock should be cured in such a way that he first destroys the shepherd with a deadly infection"? (II, 6).

In Book I Augustine made the defense of a common faith reason for treating Renatus as an equal. The bond of Catholicism unites Peter and Augustine too, but here it is cause for reproach (II,6), not an occasion for congratulation. Victor has shown himself more than ready to accept correction (II,22), and yet Peter has uncritically received what plainly ought to have been corrected. He is a Catholic, as Augustine reminds him over and over (II,5; 6; 9; 15; 17), yet he has not made use of the "rule of faith" in judging his protégé's work./17/

According to the report Augustine received, Peter enthusiastically thanked Victor for "teaching him what he did not know." This phrase becomes the unifying theme of Book II as Augustine probes Peter's reaction: Just what was it that he taught you that you did not already know? It is, of course, a loaded question. If Peter says he has just learned some article of the orthodox faith, he reveals his ignorance of teachings that surely an elderly priest ought to know. If, on the other hand, he names one of Victor's more novel ideas (e.g., that the Mass should be offered for those who die unbaptized [II,15], or that man consists of three corporeal substances: body, soul, and spirit [II,7]), he risks the charge of heresy. For example, in the first few chapters of Book II, Augustine plays question and answer: Did he teach you . . .

1) that the soul and spirit are two separate things? That is partly a matter of terminology and relatively unimportant.
2) that body and soul have different senses? Anyone knows that.
3) that the soul is a portion of God? That is heresy.
4) that the soul is corporeal? That is a matter of terminology again.
5) that the soul undergoes a judgment when the body dies? Anyone knows that.

And so the interrogation proceeds, leaving Peter with an embarrassing choice of seeming either a dunce or a heretic. One is perhaps not surprised that despite Augustine's insistence, Peter apparently never answered the letter./18/

Augustine's questioning is relentless and in Book II we see the author as polemicist. In contrast to the pastoral and collegial tone of Book I, Book II is regularly sarcastic. The central question— What did he teach you that you did not know?—undoubtedly seeks information; for the sake of church order Augustine might well wish to know just what was going on in Mauretania. But the rhetorical possibilities for playing with the theme of knowing and not-knowing and with the words *dicere-docere-discere* are irresistible.

Each question that Augustine introduces with a slight exaggeration heightens the ironic tone:

—diceris exiluisse laetitia:	You are said to have been transported with joy (II,1)
—nosse cupio:	I am longing to know (II,2)
—miror si iste te docuit:	I am astonished if this man taught you (II,3)
—gratulor eum hinc saltem:	I congratulate him on this at least (II,9).

The opening section works up to a mocking climax like a barker at a magic show:

> O doctrinam cui omnis aetas aures subrigat, quae homines annosos, quae denique presbyteros mereatur habere discipulos! Legat, legat in contione quod scripsit, notos atque ignotos, doctos atque indoctos recitaturus invitet. Seniores cum iunioribus convenite, quod nesciebatis discite, quod numquam audieratis audite! Ecce isto docente non aliunde quod aliquo modo est, nec ex eo quod omnino non est Deus flatum creat, sed ex eo quod ipse est, cum sit incorporeus, corpus sufflat!
>
> O doctrine at which every age pricks up its ears! Which deserves to have as followers men of advanced age, yes, even presbyters! Let him read, let him read in a public assembly what he has written! Let him invite to his recitation the famous and the obscure, the learned and the ignorant! Old men and young come together! Learn what you did not know! Hear what you have never heard before! See how according to this man's instruction God creates breath not from some other source which exists somehow or other, not from what does not exist at all, but from that which He Himself is, though He is incorporeal, He breathes out a corporeal entity! (II,9)

Finaert remarks that Augustine's irony is "une des formes principales de sa rhétorique" to a degree that the modern reader finds startling:

> Sans cesse nous entendons parler de la douceur et de la charité de saint Augustin envers ses amis et ses adversaires; la bienveillance était au fond du coeur, certes, mais l'expression en était souvent malicieuse et parfois cruelle. Il est difficile de trouver un rhéteur plus mordant que le "Docteur de la charité."/19/

Augustine's ironic jest then becomes deadly serious, for the distinction between Creator and created being has been violated. "Quis
hoc insanissimus opinetur?" Who could be so insane as to hold such
an opinion? Peter is sternly reminded of his Catholic faith and
blasted with a final antithetical explosion: "Absit ut hoc catholicus
animus bibat! Non enim est fluentum fontis divini sed figmentum
cordis humani."/20/ After this outburst and some more variations on
the theme "teaching you what you did not know" (II,10), Augustine
begins on a discussion of the particular errors (II,11–18) he has
found in Victor's book, the eleven enumerated in Book III and discussed above in the second chapter.

Augustine has warmed to his subject and a number of the errors
are more fully discussed than they had been in Book I. For example, Victor's assertion that "the soul through flesh deservedly recovers its primal state" is criticized at I,6 for implying that the soul
somehow deserved punishment even before it entered the flesh.
But when he criticizes the same point in Book II,11, Augustine has
realized the contradiction lurking in Victor's statements about the
soul, that he is inconsistent in representing the soul's incarnation.
For some of his pronouncements imply a soul that deserved a reward while others imply that incarnation is a punishment. Likewise
the error that unbaptized infants can obtain the kingdom of heaven
(I,6) is dealt with more fully in II,14 and 16.

This latter point is the occasion for a rather extended pun. Victor has allowed that "the principal pronouncement of Jesus stands
in the way" of allowing for salvation without baptism (quamquam
sententia illa principalis obsistat, II,16). Augustine plays on the
double sense of *principalis*, which Victor has used in its meaning of
"fundamental," and takes it also to mean "princely." Likewise *sententia*, which Victor uses as a grammatical "sentence," Augustine
turns to mean a judicial sentence. His parting shot on this question
is "Quisquis cuipiam praebet assensum adversus auctoritatem *sen-
tentiae principalis*, quam *sententiam* merebitur *principis*?" "If a
person offers his assent to someone against the authority of the
'principal sentence,' what sentence will he deserve from the
Prince?"

In addition to the fuller discussion which seems simply to come
from having had longer to think over and read over Victor's books,
Augustine adds some theological explanation most appropriate in
addressing a clerical opponent. Though the question of the soul's
relationship to God is discussed with all three correspondents, it is

only in Peter's letter compared with the question of relationships of the Trinity. Because Peter is a priest, Augustine can assume he has assimilated the orthodox position in the Arian controversy. The Council of Nicaea in 325 had defined the relationship between Father and Son as one of unity in substance (*homoousion*), or, as Augustine says in II,5, "We do not say that the Son and Holy Spirit are *part* of God" but that they are "of one and the same nature." By Augustine's time the formula μία οὐσία, τρεῖς ὑποστάσεις is the orthodox statement, usually translated as "una essentia vel substantia, tres autem personae." Gilson regards Augustine's formulation in chapter 9 as an important piece of Christological reasoning,/21/ dealing with the Son as begotten, not created, "altogether what the Father is except that He is the Son and not the Father." Because Peter is a priest, Augustine makes the demand that he, more than Victor or Renatus, be responsible for recognizing the distinction between God and created beings, for seeing that the soul must be said to be from God in a different sense than one says that Christ is from God.

Augustine also seems to assume that Peter will recognize the influence of Tertullian in Victor's assertion of the soul's corporeality (II,9). Chapter 10 alludes to another of Tertullian's points, that we resemble our parents because of a *semen animae*,/22/ a point that Victor apparently rejects. The Pelagians are also mentioned twice (II,17 and 21) as a new source of heresy, but not with the implication of their influence on Victor's group. Rather Augustine warns that the same impulse which drives the Pelagians into denying original sin altogether—the desire to save unbaptized infants from condemnation—is operating in Victor's proposal that Mass should be celebrated for the unbaptized dead; Augustine fears that Peter and Victor are thus likely to find the Pelagian solution welcome. His mention is a warning to Peter not to pursue that path any farther.

We have mentioned Augustine's outburst in II,9, a climax of irony which might well wither its object. From this point on, though the irony continues, it is more subtle, more subdued, but never lets go of Peter's astonishing (to Augustine's mind) assertion that Victor taught him what he did not know. Augustine begs to become Peter's pupil: "Me tibi docendum libentissime traderem" (II,1), but suspects that smooth talk has led the priest astray: "subrepsit tibi falsiloquium per suaviloquium." He persists in calling Victor "iste tuus doctor" (II, chs. 3,4,11,13,15, *passim*), demonstrating ever more clearly to Peter that he has let things get into the

wrong order. For though there is nothing wrong with humility before a good teacher, even a man younger than oneself (II,1), age and
authority have some natural claim to credibility and Peter ought not
to have abandoned that claim so uncritically. There is grounds for a
sympathetic bond between Peter and Augustine, for they are both
old and both priests (II,15 and 18).

Augustine is most ruefully aware
of the failings of over-cautious old men when he writes to Victor
(IV,1 and 39), but in Peter's case he wishes the old man had shown
a bit more of the usually characteristic hesitancy of the old. He
might then have seen Victor with the Bishop's eyes—as an over-
exuberant debater who has ventured out of his depth (II,11 and 17).

Just because Augustine foresees less public exposure for the
letter to Peter,/23/ he does not therefore make less use of the devices one would expect to find in an oration. The "O doctrinam"
passage of II,9 (p. 128 above) is not the only example of careful
attention to sound. At II,13 Augustine exclaims "O ammiranda
atque sectanda, immo vero detestanda et exsecranda doctrina!"/24/
At II,17 he contrasts the personifications of Veritas and Vanitas:
"contra tam *manifestas voces* quas concinit *veritas*, procedit in medium *magis vaecors* quam misericors *vanitas* et dicit. . . ." There is
a nice set of parallelisms in

> ille melior, qui emendari est paratior si non defuerit emen-
> dator, quam tu, si vel *sciens* inridenter contemnis errantem
> vel *nesciens* pariter sectaris errorem. (II,23)

Even the adverbs *inridenter* and *pariter* make up the difference in
syllables between *sciens* and *nesciens*.

Not until the last two chapters of Book II does Augustine drop
his ironic tone and become fraternal toward Peter. His last request
that the priest tell what he has learned (II,23) is an honest bid for
Peter's critical opinion, an exhortation to take seriously Victor's in-
vitation to correct him, and an encouragement of his efforts to guide
those in his charge.

The tone of the two books addressed to Victor cannot be characterized by any single quality. While irony is there, it is tempered
by an honest respect for Victor's potential as a writer and as an apologist for the faith. Augustine could certainly have felled him with
the same heavy-handed method that he reserved for Peter; that he
did not shows that his respect is genuine. While he is peeved at
being compared with cattle in ignorance, he desires Victor's understanding of his agnostic position in regard to the soul's origin and

goes to some trouble to explain more fully. He is pontifical in his warnings but disarming in his admissions of uncertainty. He can ridicule Victor's crudeness but praise his knowledge of Scripture. There is a note of humility recurring in the book, a willingness to appreciate the efforts of a fellow Christian, which is not evident in his letter to Peter./25/

In the time since he wrote to Renatus, Augustine has tried to find out more about Victor and has organized his criticism into the list of eleven errors. He begins the letter to Victor by begging that the young man will find in his writing neither the implication that he despises him nor any hope that he approves of him. The contrast describes fairly well Augustine's feelings toward Peter and Renatus respectively, though "despise" may be too strong a word even for the impatient treatment that Augustine gives Peter.

The Bishop's first question is over Victor's choice of the surname Vincentius after a Rogatist bishop. This Vincentius was an acquaintance of Augustine's from his student days and had succeeded to the office of bishop after Rogatus, the founder of the branch of Donatism bearing his name. Augustine had addressed to him around 408 a rather chilling letter justifying the use of coercion against the Donatists. The letter taunted Vincentius with the fact that his sect counted only 9 or 10 bishops. Apparently by 428, when Augustine wrote *De Haeresibus*, they had died out, since he does not mention them in the list of sects sprung from Donatism./26/

Victor's admiration for Vincentius, now dead, appears to have been directed toward his personal character rather than toward his doctrinal position, for the Rogatists demanded rebaptism of their converts whereas Victor came close to denying the necessity of baptism altogether. Nor does anything in what Augustine says to Victor imply that he regards the young man as still under the influence of characteristic Donatist teaching./27/ Augustine rejoices that Victor has been delivered from the schismatics (I,2; III,2), but the errors which he discovers in Victor's books come from other sources than Donatism. Even though Victor has renounced the errors of his former mentor, Augustine is uneasy that he should persist in considering Vincentius a holy man (III,2); "I do not want you to bear such a name as though you were the monument to a dead heretic." Even more suspicious is Victor's attribution of his works to the vision or dream of Vincentius; Augustine regards such a vision as a deception of the devil. The happy coincidence of names, Victor and Vincentius, enables Augustine to play on the derivation from *vincere*: con-

version to the Catholic faith is the real victory and the Rogatist error
lies vanquished. The extracts from Victor's writings which Augustine preserves
for us reveal Victor's enchantment with the devices of rhetoric. Passages
like the ones below tend to make one agree with Augustine's
evaluation—"*spumeosus*" (I,3)

1) (I,9) "Alia substruuntur obprobria querulis murmurationi-
   bus oblatrantum et excussi quasi quodam turbine identi-
   dem inter immania saxa conlidimur."
   Note the preponderance of liquid consonants m,n,l,r,
   especially the alternation of m and n in the last half.
2) (II,22) ". . . ne forte cuiusquam curiosi lectoris obtutus inter inlitas fibras elementorum vestigia remanentia solici-
   tent et offendant, contextam paginae seriem pollice severo
   discerpe, meque huius censionis experte, puni atramenta
   quae indigna eloquia signaverunt. . . ."
   Victor uses some rather grand vocabulary here: *inlitas
   fibras, contextam paginae seriem* (the word order is un-
   usual), *pollice* instead of *manu*, the plural of *atramentum*,
   "ink."
3) (III,11) "Anima itaque si peccatrix esse meruit, quae peccatrix esse non potuit, neque in peccato remansit, quia in
   Christo praefigurata in peccato esse non debuit, sicut esse
   non potuit."
   The writer strives for a striking effect through the use
   of paradox and repetition. Each clause ends with a perfect-
   tense verb.

Translations:

1) Other reproaches underlie the querulous murmurings of
   those who rail at us, and we are dashed about again and
   again as though by a whirlwind among huge rocks.
2) But lest the scrutiny of some curious reader should by
   chance be disturbed or offended by the surviving traces of
   elementary errors among my blurred leaves, better to tear
   apart the whole collection of pages with a relentless hand
   (literally "thumb") and, when I have undergone your criticism, punish the ink which has formed the offending
   words. . . .
3) And so, if the soul, which could not be a sinner, deserved
   to be a sinner, it still did not remain in sin, since it was
   prefigured in Christ that it was not destined to be in sin just
   as it could not be.

One of Victor's attempts at literary eloquence attracts Augustine's
sarcastic comment: "What you say about the phoenix has no relation
whatsoever to our subject . . . but I think you considered that your

discourse would draw too little applause unless you declaimed a
good deal about the phoenix in the manner of young people."/28/ I
have mentioned also the slighly mocking tone of Augustine's criticism in II,15, where Victor chooses to use the word *censeo* (see
above ch. 2, p. 68). Still, as a former teacher of rhetoric, Augustine
is not disposed to ridicule the whole enterprise, and he credits Victor with genuine ability (I,3; II,1). Books III and IV exceed I and II
in stylistic elegance, perhaps a compliment to Victor's education.

The most lyrical passage in the entire treatise is directed at
Victor in IV,8. After quoting Sirach 3:22 ("Do not inquire into what
is too high for you nor search out what is beyond your strength"),
he says:

> Neque enim altiora sunt quam potest nostra statura *contin-
> gere*, sed quam potest nostra *coniectura conprehendere* et
> fortiora quam potest vis humani ingenii penetrare; et tamen
> non est *caelum caeli*, non *dimensio siderum*, non *modus
> maris* atque terrarum, non *infernus inferior*; nos sumus qui
> nos conprehendere non valemus, nos modulum scientiae
> nostrae altiores fortioresque superamus, nos non possumus
> capere nos. . . . /29/

The parallelism of *statura contingere* with *coniectura conprehen-
dere*, the alliterations following the repeated *non . . . non . . . non*
which gives way to *nos . . . nos . . . nos* build the sense of awe at
that mystery which the *Confessions* had sought to fathom years earlier. Thus he silences what was perhaps no more than a flippant
remark of Victor's, that Augustine and the other "experts" are like
the cattle in the Psalm (48:13, LXX) who have no understanding.
So unwilling is Augustine to let that pass that he composes the longest of the four books on the question of self-knowledge, far longer
than Book III where he refutes Victor's serious points.

The length of Book IV also indicates that Augustine was really
nettled by Victor's assault on his authority. The tension evident in
Augustine's attitude toward Victor is striking. The aged Christian
knows from his own struggles and his long pastoral experience the
extreme limitations of man's knowledge and the precariousness of
his faith./30/ Thus Augustine is not merely being polite when he
declines Victor's complimentary (though perhaps ironic) adjectives,
doctissimus and *peritissimus* (IV,1) and affects humility (IV,39; I,2).
Yet the brashness of the young man galls him too, and he cannot
resist going him one better, for example in his little summary of
anatomical science (IV,3–6), his aside that Victor has either got a

bad memory or a bad text (III,7) when he brings in the Elisha story, or his description of a scientific experiment proving that air is a substance (IV,18). Much of Augustine's argumentation is simply taking Victor's points or methods and pressing them to the breaking point. In IV,28, where Victor has asserted that the soul retains the shape of the body yet withdraws from an injured or amputated part so as not to share in the injury, Augustine shows the absurdity by positing the case of an old man with an arm amputated in infancy: will his soul then bear one infant's arm and one old man's arm? With some slightly ribald observations (IV,32–33), Augustine wryly exposes the hopeless inconsistency of Victor's denial that the soul has a sex even though it conforms to the shape of the physical body. Victor wishes to prove the soul's corporeality from the rich man's recognition of Lazarus in the bosom of Abraham. Augustine sarcastically asks him whether he runs to the mirror every few hours to keep from losing his recognition of himself (IV,21).

Augustine consents to argue with Victor on his own ground, whether he thinks it well-chosen or not. Victor uses Dinocrates, the brother of St. Perpetua, as an example of a child saved through intercession and not baptism (III,12). After rejecting that argument, Augustine nevertheless goes on to make use of the history of St. Perpetua for two other proofs *against* Victor's assertions (see IV,26 and 27). It is as though he says, "You want to use the *Passio Perpetuae* as evidence? All right, I will use it as evidence against you." He wants to argue on Victor's own ground even though he personally thinks one ought not to argue matters of doctrine from noncanonical sources (III,12). Likewise he does not scold Victor for reading the Montanist Tertullian but does congratulate him for rejecting Tertullian's "madness" in thinking God corporeal (II,10; IV,18); he also makes it clear that he is familiar with Tertullian's *De Anima* and treats its author seriously./31/

Victor believed that his arguments could be supported from Scripture. Augustine spends a large portion of Book I (15 chapters out of 35) examining those texts, another illustration of his willingness to meet an opponent on his own ground. But he is able to show in each case that either the text is ambiguous and would not exclude a traducianist interpretation or that its meaning is distorted by Victor's too-literal reading. Nevertheless Augustine admits Victor's commendable acquaintance with Scripture (III,21) though he lacks something in experience and judgment ("eruditio minor est quam tantae indoli laborique congruebat). Augustine's careful criticism of his Scriptural texts shows the teacher at work, demonstrating to his pupil the principles of interpretation that he had worked out earlier in *De Doctrina Christiana*, Books I-III.

Augustine wishes to instruct Victor, but one wonders if it is his own disastrous experience with cruel schoolmasters that leads him to speak very gently when he speaks as a teacher:

> Nec ideo tamen te contemnas et arbitreris ingenium et eloquium tuum parvi esse pendendum. . . . Itaque te nec amplius quam oportet tibi tribuendo vanescere volo, nec rursus te abiciendo ac desperando frigescere. Utinam tua scripta tecum legere possem et conloquendo potius quam scribendo quae sint emendanda monstrarem! Facilius hoc negotium perageretur nostra inter nos sermocinatione quam litteris. . . . /32/

He is concerned that his criticisms should not leave his opponent crushed and discouraged nor cause him to doubt his real ability. The longing for the intimacy of conversation rather than the cold formality of letter-writing recalls the setting of his early writings from Cassiciacum, where the distinction between teacher and student receded before the ideal of listening to the divine Teacher. In his closing chapter Augustine deliberately puts aside the teacher/pupil image altogether and replaces it with a moving reminder of his old age:

> . . . venire tibi non sit onerosum, non tamquam discipulo ad magistrum, sed primaevo ad grandaevum, forti ad infirmum./33/

As a writer, Victor will himself be a teacher of others, and Augustine reminds him what his real task will be:

> Quapropter ut et tu recte sapias et alios non tantummodo delectare possit, verum etiam aedificare quod loqueris, curam te oportet gerere de sermonibus tuis, remotis plausibus alienis./34/

Victor never presented the threat to the Church that Pelagius or Julian of Eclanum did; many of his errors were crude ones, and his partiality toward Tertullian linked him to a materialism long out of fashion in Christian thought./35/ Yet Augustine took him seriously and the mixture of harsh polemic with mild admonition and even tenderness is not so different from the tone of the anti-Pelagian treatises.

This small episode in the North African Church reveals that Augustine took account of personalities even when his writings were all necessarily designed to become public property. His friendly gratitude toward Renatus, his harsh irony toward Peter, and his paternal chastening of Vincentius Victor make the books of DNOA more than a mere recital of errors and their refutations. Augustine is not afraid to reveal his opinions about his correspondents. He had already lived through the storms of criticism over the *Confessions*, which some churchmen regarded as scandalous for its candid expositions of the author's uncertainties and sins, and the experience had not convinced him that it would be wiser to dissimulate. He accepts the ground on which his adversary wishes to argue but either turns the arguments back against him or else reduces them to absurdity. His opponent presents an easy target, but Augustine chooses to reserve his stiffest blows for Victor's patron as bearing a greater responsibility for the errors.

Augustine sees Victor variously as an upstart, a promising natural talent, a potential heretic, a future champion of the faith, a pupil, a son, a babbler, a gifted rhetor, a naive provincial, a representative of a possibly troublesome party, the butt of ridicule, an object of paternal love. All this the Bishop does in a style recognized in his time as masterful. Examples of these styles have been given, and they conform wonderfully in practice to the theory he set out in *De Doctrina Christiana*:

> Just as the listener is to be delighted if he is to be retained as a listener, so also he is to be persuaded if he is to be moved to act. And just as he is delighted if you speak sweetly, so is he persuaded if he loves what you promise, fears what you threaten, hates what you condemn, embraces what you commend, sorrows at what you maintain to be sorrowful, rejoices when you announce something delightful, takes pity on those whom you place before him in speaking as being pitiful, flees those whom you, moving fear, warn are to be avoided; and is moved by whatever else may be done through grand eloquence toward moving the minds of listeners. . . . (LLA)/36/

If Victor is a wandering sheep, Augustine is the conscientious shepherd. But one cannot help comparing him also to the sheepdog snapping at the heels of the stray, threatening, pushing, occasionally drawing blood in his determination to drive his charge out of danger and back into the fold.

NOTES

/1/   See chapter 1, p. 16 and p. 29.

/2/   *L'Évolution littéraire de St. Augustin* (Paris: Société d'Édition "Les Belles Lettres," 1939) p. 139.

/3/   Both of those questions remain lively issues within the Church up to the present time and constitute one reason for the present denominational divisions. Discussion of "the soul," on the other hand, appears to be limited to theologians.

/4/   See *Ep.* 190 and Introduction, above, p. 5.

/5/   e.g., I,2: I,31.

/6/   See *Ad Orosium liber unus*, PL 42, 667–668.

/7/   Marrou (*Augustin et la fin* . . . , p. 90) contrasts our modern criterion for speeches with the standards of antiquity. We tend to think of how a speech would look in print. The listener from Augustine's time would judge even a written work by how it would *sound*. See also ch. 1 above on the relation of written to spoken word, pp. 21–22.

/8/   Augustine even cites Mk. 16:18, "Even if they drink any deadly thing, it will not hurt them," as evidence that heresy is ultimately powerless (II,23). The faith in the power of truth is comparable to the Christian idea of the role of the preacher: he is personally unimportant and a mere instrument in the hands of the true Teacher. See ch. 1, pp. 27–28.

/9/   See *Ep.* 190 and Introduction, above, p. 5.

/10/   In *Retr.* II,56, Augustine makes a distinction between Bks. I and II, calling the first a treatise (*liber*) and the second a letter (*epistula*), though they are roughly the same length. He does not explain what the difference is, but the more personal character of II with its many requests to Peter for a reply may show that he did not expect a wider circulation for it. In II,14, Augustine recommends to Peter that he get hold of the treatise to Renatus, and in III,3, he says the same to Victor.

/11/   I,3. The quotations in these two paragraphs come from I,3 also.

/12/   In *De Cat. Rud.* of 405, I,8,12, Augustine commends the "marvelous sublimity joined to most wholesome simplicity" of the Scriptures and contrasts that with other literature, which boasts "a style of more sonorous and neatly-turned expression adapted, according to each writer's ability, to prouder, and therefore weaker, minds" (ACW trans., p. 31). The link of pride to weakness illustrates the value attached to *humilitas*; see ch. 1, pp. 22–24.

/13/   Augustine admits his fondness for rhythmical and rhyming clauses in DDC IV,20,41. For a study of his style with statistical information on the kinds of *clausulae*, see Patristic Studies, vols. 6, 7, and 88, for the rhetoric of the sermons, CD, and *De Natura Boni* (PL 42) respectively.

/14/   This latter looks like a proverb or at least an adaptation of a proverb. At II,23, Augustine uses "in pretioso poculo" again and connects the picture of drinking poison from a precious cup with Mk. 16:18, "Even if they drink any deadly thing it will not hurt them."

/15/   Let him tell whether what [the soul] deserved is something good or evil. If good, why did evil result from merit? If evil, where could any demerit come from before any sin? Likewise I [must] add: if [the soul deserves] good, then the grace which liberates it is not free but [simply] the payment of a debt which positive merits preceded, and in that case 'grace is no longer grace'; on the other hand, if [the soul deserves] evil, I [must] ask what that [evil] is: Is it that it has come into the flesh, where it would never have come unless that One had sent it in whom there is no injustice?" (I,9)

/16/   De Veer thinks it possible that Peter might have converted Victor from the Rogatists to Catholicism, "Aux origines . . . ," p. 123.

/17/   "*Ecclesiastica regula*" (I,13) or "*regula fidei*" (II,23) is that rule established in Scripture; where Scripture is unspecific, the rule is what the Church has always done (e.g., baptized infants). For Augustine there is no question of two different sources, Scripture and Tradition, as one finds in Reformation theology. There is one Truth, the Word of God, who speaks through the prophets and Biblical writers or through Apostles and leaders of the Church. Tradition is simply the extension of that one voice. See "Règle de foi et tradition," BA 22, pp. 788–790, n. 36.

/18/   *Retr.* II,56 mentions an answer from Victor but not Peter.

/19/   *Saint Augustin rhéteur* (Paris: Société des études latines, 1939). p. 66.

/20/   "Heaven forbid that a Catholic mind should imbibe such [an idea]. For that is no stream from a divine source but a figment of the human imagination." The same mixture of heavy sarcasm and thunderous condemnation is found in another letter to a priest, to Vincentius the Rogatist (*Ep.* 93), the same Vincentius whose name Victor had adopted. Note another drinking metaphor.

/21/   p. 87. Also p. 301, n. 133.

/22/   Tertullian *De An.* 5,4. The similarity of children to parents is presented by Tertullian as proof that the soul is corporeal. He attributes the argument to Cleanthes and in 25,9 brings it up again as proof of a *semen animae*. Whether Victor accepted that notion or not hinges on a translation difficulty. The Latin of 11,10 reads, "Quod autem similitudines morum, qui repperiuntur in filiis, non ex animae semine venire disputat, consequens est. . . ." The problem is whether *non* belongs with *disputat* (PNF) or with *venire* (BA, Fingerle, and De Veer).

/23/   He intends at least Victor to see it (III,3).

/24/   Mss. BCFG omit the second half, and PNF follows them. BA, however, retains the reading above.

/25/   We might compare his generous words about Pelagius himself in *De Peccatorum Meritis* III,1 and 5 (PL 44), where even with the man's writings at hand, he is ready to believe the reports that this opponent is "a good and praiseworthy man," "a holy man, as I am told." *Ep.* 186 also tells his feelings for Pelagius.

/26/   *Ep.* 93, trans. FOC 18, pp. 56–106. More on the Rogatists in W. H. C. Frend, *The Donatist Church* (Oxford: Clarendon, 1952), pp. 197. ff.

/27/   Augustine's complete lack of anti-Donatist polemic against Victor, other than the disapproval of his surname, suggests that Frend is justified in treating the Donatist movement as less a theological dispute than a matter of regional or cultural loyalties. Not that the two can be entirely separated, especially in the case of Donatism, where the heart of the dispute is the nature of the Church, whether it is to be worldwide or the possession of a few. *Ep.* 93 is a good illustration of the difference in outlook: for Augustine the Church is defined as necessarily καθολική and cannot therefore be confined just to Mauretania or even Africa. For Vincentius the very exclusivity of his sect is the guarantee of its authenticity.

/28/   One is reminded of the chorus in A. E. Housman's parody, "Fragment of a Greek Tragedy," the stanza which begins "Why should I mention Io?", goes on to recount her story, and closes with "Why should I mention Io? Why indeed? I do not have the faintest notion why."

/29/   "Not that they are too high for our physical stature to reach but rather for our thought to encompass, and beyond the strength of human intelligence to penetrate. Yet it is not the heaven of heavens, not the measure of the stars, not the bounds of sea or land, not the lowest depths that we lack the power to comprehend; it is ourselves. We surpass the modest scope of our own knowledge; we are the 'too high' and the 'too strong'; we cannot grasp ourselves. . . . "

/30/   His last finished work, *De Dono Perseverantiae* (PL 45), written in 429, was a last witness to what he saw as the necessity of God's action in faith. As grace alone enabled man to come to faith in the first place, so grace alone enabled him to persevere to the end in faith.

/31/   J. H. Waszink, *Quinti Florentii Tertulliani de anima* (Amsterdam: Meulenhoff, 1947), p. 48, says "The only author who was really influenced by Tertullian's psychological theses is Vincentius Victor," but thinks Augustine was "well-acquainted with the contents of *De anima*." For the specific points on which Tertullian influences Victor, see De Veer, "Aux origines . . . ," pp. 146–147. Tertullian thought the similarity of children to their parents proved that the soul was inherited and that it was corporeal. Victor thought it was corporeal but rejected Tertullian's traducianism. Augustine points out in II,10 that even if souls are inherited through propagation, children may be unlike their parents in disposition. One can make a case for their being like or unlike, but traducianism is not the necessary inference from either opinion.

/32/   III,21. "Nevertheless, do not despise yourself or think that your talent and eloquence are of little value. . . . And so I neither wish you to grow vain by crediting yourself with more than you should, nor do I want you to become paralyzed by dejection and despair. If only I could read your writings with you and show you in conversation rather than in writing what should be corrected! This business could be accomplished far more easily by discussion between us than by letters."

/33/   IV,39. "[I pray that] it will not be burdensome for you to come to me—not as a pupil to a teacher but as a man in his prime to an old man, a strong man to a weak one."

/34/   IV,39. "Therefore in order that you may become truly wise and that what you say may have power not only to delight but to edify, you ought to exercise care in your speech, discounting the applause of others."

/35/   The belief in a corporeal soul was seriously defended as late as 470 by Claudianus Mamertus, see E. L. Fortin, *Christianisme et culture philosophique*. But Spanneut documents a decline in the influence of Stoicism on Christian writers after 230 (pp. 63–74) and a gradual ascendancy of Neoplatonic ideas on the soul.

/36/   IV,27. This part of the treatise was not written until 427, after a lifetime of rhetorical exercise in sermonizing and writing. Augustine's basis of effective rhetoric is still Cicero's triad: to instruct, to please, and to persuade (*Orator* XXI,69).

SUMMARY AND CONCLUSION

I have attempted in this dissertation first of all simply to provide a study of a work that has not attracted much scholarly attention for reasons enumerated in the Introduction above. DNOA is clearly a minor work by comparison with the *City of God* or the *Confessions* or *De Trinitate*; yet in the preceding chapters the reader has been shown the relation of this treatise to a number of major issues in Augustinian studies: the early Christian attitude toward rhetoric, the soul's creation and its powers, the nature of sin, and the theory of knowledge. Volumes have been written on each of these subjects (a rather large number of them by Augustine himself), but DNOA shows the principles of the Bishop's great scholarly treatises worked out on the smaller scale of a local controversy.

DNOA illustrates Augustine's continued and ever-expanding interest in the art of rhetoric. Though his education had prepared him well for the public life thrust on him as a Catholic convert, he went through a period of disillusionment with that education and its goals. Following the example of earlier serious-minded pagans and Christians, he turned his back on rhetoric for a time to embrace a life of philosophical contemplation. But the demands made on his talent and the imperative of community inherent in Christian theology recalled him to an active life where his words would influence masses of people. As he was drawn back into public speaking and writing, he was necessarily drawn into reconsideration of the art of rhetoric. *De Doctrina Christiana* is the ultimate product of that reconsideration. Books I-III deal with Scriptural interpretation, with written language, one could also say with the contemplative part of the Christian life. Book IV, written 31 years later, deals with instruction and persuasion, that is, the active life that grows out of the contemplative.

DNOA, written 419–420, predates the last book of *De Doctrina* by about seven years, but I have shown by the frequent citations of *De Doctrina* how Augustine's thinking regarding the art of persuasion had already matured by this time. DNOA illustrates amply many of the principles of *De Doctrina*—for example: the *officia oratoris* of Cicero, viz., that the teacher or orator should instruct, please, and move his listener; the attention to appropriateness of arguments and style to one's audience; and the conviction that Christian rhetoric has a peculiar urgency in that it deals with matters of eternal import. Chapter 1 examined the classical and the Biblical foundations of Augustine's thought on rhetoric, with attention to the respects in which those traditions sometimes coincided and sometimes differed. Although at the time he wrote the *Confessions* Augustine understood his own conversion as a turning away from the central study of his Roman education, later he could openly acknowledge the validity of rhetorical training for a Christian; one could press rhetoric into the service of God. And although the Augustine of the *Confessions* exalted philosophy over rhetoric as an appropriate profession for a Christian, the later Augustine realized that both rhetoric and philosophy were vulnerable to the same temptation, viz., *superbia*.

Vincentius Victor, Augustine's opponent, had succumbed to that temptation both as a philosopher and as a rhetorician. His most dangerous error, to Augustine's mind, was seeming to say that the soul was a particle of God, and he claimed certainty on an issue (the origin of the soul) concerning which neither reason nor Scripture justified such confidence. As a writer, he seemed to the Bishop of Hippo to prize applause above sober efforts to find the truth. The sequence of chapters in this dissertation may be seen, from one point of view, as corresponding to these manifestations of *superbia*. The most serious error, of those eleven examined in Chapter 2, was Victor's tendency toward identifying the soul with God. Victor's error, like Adam's primal sin, blurred the distinction between Creator and creature. Besides that principal error, Victor's opinions on baptism seemed to Augustine to reflect arrogance toward the authority of the Church and its traditions. Chapters 3 and 4 showed how Victor's claim to certainty was also a kind of *superbia*, a refusal both to admit that certain things might lie beyond human understanding and to confess his ignorance of his own self. Not only were there plenty of Scriptural warnings against claiming complete knowledge (and thus again, like Adam, grasping at a divine prerogative), but classical wisdom, as represented by the sayings "knowing what you do not know" and "know thyself," cautioned against pride. Finally, in his very language Victor, in Augustine's opinion, abandoned the moderation appropriate both to his youth and to a genuine theological inquiry. Although the Bishop saw promise in his young antagonist, he was offended by the arrogant tone of his work; Chapter 5 examined Augustine's response thereto—a response at once encouraging and admonishing.

Augustine's approach to Victor was not simply to thunder at him with words from Scripture (although there is some of that in DNOA) but to combine appeals to faith and reason. On the question of baptism, Scripture and the Church's tradition were, of course, the decisive authority, but even the arguments involving dogma were refuted as often by Augustine's showing their faulty logic as by his quoting Biblical authority. This complementary relationship of faith to reason in Augustine's thinking is apparent too in what he says about knowledge and ignorance in DNOA. It is no surprise that he admitted a point at which *ratio* gives out; what is perhaps unexpected is that he did not then jump in with an answer from *auctoritas* but accepted a state of uncertainty on a question that many Christians of his time regarded as enormously important to have settled. Yet his agnostic stance on the origin of the soul was not Academic scepticism but rather a sort of *humilitas*, the one element he had found lacking in the philosophers he most admired. Thus DNOA offers an enlightening study of Augustine's method of searching for truth, in other words, of Augustine's practice of φιλοσοφία.

Even though such controversies as the one in Mauretania kept Augustine from the philosophic life which he had first envisioned as a Christian convert, nevertheless his passion for wisdom survived undiminished. The demands on his rhetorical skill did not force him to abandon φιλοσοφία; on the contrary, they fired his teacher's imagination for the task of pointing others toward the "true philosophy." Augustine never credited himself or any other human teacher with the power to convert: that power belonged only to the Holy Spirit, the Inner Teacher. But he did recognize the power of speech to delight the hearer and move him toward receptivity. That is why he offered Victor criticism on his rhetorical style as well as on his opinions. And that is why he himself took such pains to answer Victor with care and seriousness—and with occasional humor and verbal brilliance. For Augustine had always before him a pastoral purpose: to guide his opponent from heresy to "saving knowledge."

APPENDIX A

Book III of
De Natura Et Origine Animae

1. In writing what I thought must be written to you, my dearest son Victor, I want you first of all to consider this: if I despised you I would not have undertaken to do it at all. On the other hand, do not abuse my humility so much that you think you are approved just because you perceive that you are not despised. For I love you not as someone who is to be followed but as someone who is to be corrected. And since I am not without hope that you can be corrected, do not marvel that I cannot despise one whom I love. For if, before you were of our communion, it was my duty to love you in order that you might become a Catholic, how much more, now that you have become one of us, must I love you so that you may not be a new heretic but rather be such a Catholic as no heretic could stand up against! For as is evident from the gifts of intelligence which God has already poured out on you, you will undoubtedly be a wise man if only you do not consider yourself so, and if you piously, humbly, and earnestly beseech from that One who makes men wise that you may be so, and if you prefer not being deceived by error to being honored by the praise of erring men.

2. The heading of your name on your books first aroused my concern on your behalf. For when I inquired who Vincentius Victor was from those who knew you and happened to be present, I heard that you had been a Donatist, or rather a Rogatist, but had recently joined the Catholic Church. I rejoiced as greatly as we usually do over those whom we learn have been freed from that error, indeed even more, because I saw that your intelligence which pleased me in your writings no longer remained at the disposal of the adversaries of truth. And yet something which saddened me in the midst of that joy was added by my informants, viz., that you had wished to

be surnamed Vincentius because you still esteemed Rogatus' successor, who was called by this name, as a great and holy man, and for this reason you wished his name to be your surname.

There were even those who claimed that you boasted that he himself had appeared to you in some sort of vision and had so assisted you in the composition of the books which I have undertaken to discuss with you in this work of mine, that he dictated to you what ought to be written regarding the very topics and arguments. If that is true, I am not surprised that you were able to say things which, if you will patiently attend to my admonition and consider and think over those books with the mind of a Catholic, I have no doubt you will regret having said. For he who, as the apostle says of him "transforms himself into an angel of light," was transformed for you into the one whom you think was or is like an angel of light [viz. the older Vincentius]. And certainly in this shape, viz., when he transforms himself not into angels of light but into heretics, he is less able to deceive Catholics; but I would wish that you would not be deceived by him now that you are a Catholic. May his torment at your learning what is true be even greater than the joy he once felt at having persuaded you of what was false.

However, in order that you may not give your love to a dead man (a love which can hinder you and cannot help him), I urge you to consider this briefly: certainly he is not holy and just if you have escaped the snares of the Donatist, or Rogatist, heretics. But if you think him holy and just, it is you who are lost by communing with Catholics. For plainly you [only] pretend to be a Catholic if you are of the same mind as that one whom you admire. And you know how frighteningly it is written [in Scripture] "The holy spirit of instruction will flee from the pretender." If, however, you are sincere in your communion with us and do not [merely] pretend to be a true Catholic, why do you still esteem a dead heretic so much that you wish to boast of his name while no longer held by his error? I do not want you to bear such a surname, as though you were a monument of a dead heretic; I do not want your book to have such a title as we would call false if we should read it on his gravestone. For we know that Vincentius ["the conquering one"] is not the victor but the vanquished. And would that [he were vanquished] for his own good just as I wish you to be vanquished by the truth.

Yet it is a clever ploy on your part to attribute to Vincentius Victor those books of yours, which you want people to believe were dictated to you by him; you seem to wish not so much that you

should be called Vincent as that he should be called Victor, as
though by revealing to you what you should write he had won a
victory over error. Why do you hold these [views], my son? Be a
true Catholic rather than a feigned one, lest the Holy Spirit flee
from you and you get no profit from Vincentius, into whom a most
malignant spirit transformed himself in order to deceive you; for
these [opinions] are his, by whatever fraud he persuaded you.

If, on this admonition, you correct those views in sincere humility and Catholic peace, your errors will be judged those of a
youth more zealous to receive correction than eager to remain in
error. If, however, you are persuaded (God forbid!) to defend them
obstinately, then it will be necessary to condemn the teachings,
along with their author, as heretical albeit with the concern of a
pastor and physician, before frightful contagion creeps through the
unwary people when wholesome discipline is disregarded in the
semblance of love, though not its reality.

3. If you ask what these [heretical doctrines] are, you will
doubtless be able to read what I have written to our brothers Renatus, the servant of God, and Peter, the priest. To the latter you felt
should be written these very same matters which we are discussing,
"submitting to his will since he requested it," as you state. I have
no doubt that they will give you my letters to read if you wish, and
even if you do not ask, they will press them on you. Nevertheless,
even here I will not remain silent concerning what I most wish to
be amended in those same books of yours and in your faith.

The first point is this: you affirm that "the soul is created by
God in such a way that He made it from Himself rather than from
nothing." On this point you do not think it follows necessarily that
the soul is of the nature of God, since even you yourself recognize
how impious that would be. To avoid that impiety you must maintain that God is the Creator of the soul in such a way that it was
made *by* Him, not *from* Him. For what is from Him, as is the only-
begotten Son, is of the same nature as He is. But since the soul is
not of the same nature as He is, it was in truth made by Him but
not from Him. Therefore, either tell me where it comes from or
else confess that it is made from nothing. What do you mean when
you say: "The soul is a particle of the breath of God's nature"? Do
you really deny that that "breath of God's nature"—a breath which
includes this particle—is of the same nature as God? If you deny
this, it follows that God made from nothing even that breath of
which you claim that the soul is a particle.

On the other hand, if [this breath] is not from nothing, tell where God did make it from. If [He made it] from Himself, then He is, heaven forbid, the material principle [*materies*] of His own work. But you say: "When He makes breath or exhalation [*halitus vel flatus*] from Himself, He remains whole"—as though the flame of a lamp did not remain whole when another is lit from it, and yet this flame is of the same nature, not a different one.

4. "But," you say, "when we blow up a balloon, it is not some portion of our nature or our quality that we blow into it, since this expansion of the inflated balloon by the indrawn air happens without our being in the least diminished." You keep enlarging on this argument, both emphasizing and insisting on the illustration as a necessary one for our understanding of how God makes the soul from Himself without any damage to His own nature, yet though it is made from Him, it is not what He is. You ask: "Is the air which inflates a balloon a part of our soul? Or do we fashion human beings when we blow up balloons? Or do we experience any detriment to ourselves when we disperse our breath in various directions? No, we experience none when we transmit our breath from ourselves to some other object; and since there remains in us the full quality and undiminished quantity of our own breath, we are aware that we feel no loss from the inflating of a balloon." This illustration appears elegant and suitable enough to you, but look how wrong you are. What you say is that the incorporeal God breathes out a corporeal soul not made by Him from nothing but from His own self, whereas the air that *we* breathe out (corporeal, but of a finer quality than our bodies) we do not exhale from our souls but from the air, through the internal organs of the body. In fact it is the soul, at whose bidding the other members of the body are also moved, which moves the lungs to this drawing and expelling of breaths of air like a bellows.

For in addition to the solid and liquid aliments, from which we get food and drink, God has poured out around us this third aliment, the air. This is so necessary to us that, though we can exist without food and drink for some time, without this third aliment which the surrounding air offers us as we inhale and exhale, we cannot live for even a short period of time. Moreover, just as food and drink must not only be ingested but also expelled through the channels created for that purpose so that they may not do harm in any direction, either by not coming in or not going out, so also this third aliment, the air, since it is not allowed to stay in us or to be corrupted by remaining inside but is expelled as soon as it is taken in, has received not different channels but the same ones for going in and out, namely the mouth or the nostrils or both.

5. Prove for yourself, and in yourself, what I say. Let out a breath and see whether you can last if you do not breathe in again; breathe in and see what distress you feel if you do not breathe out again. Now, what we do when we blow up a balloon (as you say) is what we do to stay alive, except that in the former case we inhale a little harder in order to exhale harder and force the flow of air, that is the wind, into the balloon that is to be filled and distended, not by quietly inhaling and exhaling but by the force of hard breathing. So how can you claim that "we experience no detriment when we transmit our breath from ourselves to some other object, and since there remains in us the full quality and undiminished quantity of our own breath, we are aware that we feel no loss from the inflating of a balloon"? It appears, my son, that if you have ever inflated a balloon, you have not paid attention to what you were doing. For you do not perceive what you lose by breathing out since you regain it immediately. But you can learn this very easily if your real desire is [to learn] it rather than to defend what you have said [merely] because you have already said it—not inflating balloons but inflated yourself—and to inflate your hearers with the empty roar of long-winded talk when you ought to be building them up with true facts.

In this matter I send you to no teacher except yourself. Blow your breath into a balloon. Close your mouth at once and hold your nostrils shut and in this way, finally, discover that what I say is true. For when you begin to endure unbearable distress, what is it that you wish to recover with your open mouth and nostrils, if you think that when you breathed out you lost nothing? Look what a bad state you would be in if you did not regain by inhaling what you had emitted by exhaling; look what loss and harm that inhalation would have caused if it had not been compensated for by respiration. For unless what you expended for expanding [*inpenderis . . . implendum*] the balloon likewise returns for your sustenance through an open channel, what will you have left, not just for blowing up a balloon, but for enabling you to live?

6. You ought to have considered all this when you wrote and not, in the illustration of inflated or inflateable balloons, to have presented us with [those ideas of yours: viz.,] that God either breathed out souls from another nature which already existed, just as we produce our breath from the surrounding air, or (what is both

inconsistent with your illustration and replete with impiety) that God, without any detriment to Himself but nevertheless from His own nature either put forth something mutable or, worse yet, created as though He were Himself the material cause [*materies*] of His own work. But in order that we may draw some [useful] comparison on this matter from our breathing, we ought rather to believe the following: that just as we, though alive and sentient, produce breath that is neither living nor sentient, not from our own nature but (since we are not omnipotent) from the surrounding air which we draw in and discharge when we inhale and exhale, so God is able to make breath that is both living and sentient, albeit mutable (though He Himself is immutable) not from His own nature but, because He is so omnipotent that He can create what He wants, even from that which altogether *is not*, that is, from nothing.

7. But why did you think it necessary to add to this comparison as an example the case of the blessed Elisha: to wit, that he revived a dead person by breathing into his face? Do you really think that the breath of Elisha was made the soul of the boy? I cannot believe you are so far off the right track. Now if that very soul, which had been removed from the living person so that he died, was returned to him so that he revived, how is what you said pertinent to the case, viz., "Elisha was not in any way diminished"? It is as though one were to think that something was transferred from him to the boy which caused the boy to live! If your reason for having said it is that he breathed and [yet] remained whole, what need was there to talk about Elisha reviving a dead person when you could say the same of anyone who breathes but revives no one. Indeed you carelessly said (though heaven forbid you should believe that the breath of Elisha became the soul of the revived boy) that you wished to distinguish the act of God from the act of the prophet principally by this fact: that God breathed only once, Elisha three times. You actually made Elisha's breathing into the face of the Shunamite's son a figure of [man's] primeval origin. You stated: "And when divine strength through the breath of the prophet aroused his dead limbs, revivified in their original vigor, Elisha was in no way diminished, through whose breath the corpse received a revived soul and spirit. The only difference was that the Lord breathed once into the face of man and he lived whereas Elisha breathed three times into the face of the dead person and he lived again." You make it sound as though the number of breaths were the only difference which would keep us from believing that what God has done the prophet

has done too. This, then, must be corrected. So great, in fact, was the difference between God's work and Elisha's that God breathed the breath of life by which man was made into a living soul; Elisha, however, breathed a breath neither sentient nor living but figurative for the sake of signifying something. In short, the prophet did not cause the boy to revive by enlivening [*animando*] him; but by loving [*amando*] him he prevailed on God to bring it about. (As for your saying he breathed three times: either your memory—as often happens—or an error in your text has deceived you.)

Why say more? You ought not to invent more examples or arguments for proving your point but rather to change and correct your opinion. Therefore, do not believe, do not say, do not teach that "God made the soul from His own nature, rather than from nothing."

8. Do not believe, or say, or teach that "through infinite time and always God gives souls, even as He who gives always exists," if you wish to be a Catholic. For a time will come when God will not give souls, although he Himself will, nevertheless, not cease to exist. Certainly, your words "always gives" could be taken in such a way that God would be understood to give without ceasing, so long as human beings generate and are generated, as it has been said of some: "always learning and never arriving at a knowledge of the truth." For here the word "always" is not to be understood as meaning they never cease to learn, since obviously they will not [continue to] learn when they cease to live in this body or when they begin to burn with the punishment of hellfire. But you have not allowed your word to be taken in this way when you said "always gives," since plainly you thought this should refer to infinite time. And that was not enough; but as though you had been asked to explain more clearly the sense in which you said "always gives," you added the clause: "even as He who gives always exists." This [assertion] a wholesome and Catholic faith rejects altogether. For heaven forbid we should believe that "God always gives souls, even as He who gives always exists." True, He always exists in that He never ceases to exist; He will not, however, always give souls but will assuredly cease to give them when the age of generation is finished and there are no longer any being born to whom souls must be given.

9. Do not believe or say or teach that "the soul lost some merit through [being incarnated in] flesh" as though it had good merit before [its incarnation in] flesh, if you wish to be a Catholic. For the

apostle says that those not yet born have done nothing either good
or evil. Therefore how could the soul before [putting on] flesh have
had good merits, when it had done nothing good? Or will you perhaps dare to say that it lived well previous to [life in] the flesh when
you cannot show that it even existed? How can you then say [to
me]: "You do not wish the soul to draw its condition from sinful flesh
when you see that sanctification is in turn transferred to it through
flesh so that it regains its [healthy] state through the same [means]
by which it lost its merit"? In case you are unaware of it, these
doctrines, in which the soul is considered to have had some good
state or good merits before [life in the] flesh, the Catholic Church
has already condemned, more recently among the Priscillianists,
not to mention earlier heretics.

10. Do not believe or say or teach that "the soul through flesh
is restored to its primal state and is reborn through that [means] by
which it had deserved to be defiled," if you wish to be a Catholic. I
leave aside that where you say: "Therefore through the flesh [the
soul] deservedly recovers its primal state which it seemed to have
lost for a time through the flesh, so that it begins to be reborn
through that [means] by which it had deserved to be defiled," you
have plainly contradicted yourself in such a short space that you first
say the soul recovers its [former] state through flesh by which it had
lost merit (where 'merit' can not be understood as anything else
than good merit [*bonum meritum*], which you indeed claim is restored through flesh in baptism); then you turn around and assert
that it has deserved to be defiled through flesh (where its deserts
can not now be understood as a good merit but as an evil merit
[*malum meritum*].) But to leave this [contradiction] aside, it is quite
simply not Catholic to believe that the soul had either good or bad
merit before it became incarnate.

11. Do not believe or say or teach that "the soul deserved to be
a sinner before any sin," if you wish to be a Catholic. For certainly
it is a bad merit [*malum meritum*] to have deserved being made a
sinner. And obviously it could not have had such a bad merit before
[it had committed] any sin, especially not before it had entered into
flesh when it could have deserved neither good nor ill. How can
you then say: "And so, if the soul, which could not be a sinner,
deserved to be a sinner, it still did not remain in sin, since it was
prefigured in [the case of] Christ that it must not be in sin, just as
it could not be"? Watch what you are saying and cease to say it from
now on. For how could [the soul] deserve to be, but not be able to

be, a sinner? How, I ask you, did [a soul] which had never led a bad life deserve to be a sinner? How, I ask you, was that made a sinner which could not be a sinner? Or if you mean "could not" in the sense that it could not [sin] apart from the flesh, how then did [the soul] deserve to be a sinner and to be sent as its just deserts into flesh, when actually it could not have been a sinner before its incarnation or have merited any evil from that [earlier state]?

12. Do not believe or say or teach that "infants who die before they can be baptized can obtain forgiveness of their original sin," if you wish to be a Catholic. For the examples which deceive you—that of the thief who on the cross confessed the Lord, or of Dinocrates, the brother of Saint Perpetua—do not support your erroneous opinion at all. Indeed, although that thief could by divine judgment be reckoned among those who are purified by the confession of martyrdom, nevertheless you do not even know whether he might not have been baptized. For, not to mention the belief that the one crucified with Christ could have had poured over him the water mixed with blood which gushed from the Lord's side and been washed by a most holy baptism in this way, what if he had been baptized in prison, which even in a later time of persecution some were able to accomplish secretly? What if [he had been baptized] even before his arrest? (For the public laws could not for that reason spare him as far as the death of the body was concerned just because he had received remission of sins at God's hand.) What if already baptized he had fallen into the sin and crime of robbery and, not as an unbaptized person but as a penitent, accepted the pardon for his crimes committed after his baptism? It is at this point that his trusting faith appeared to the Lord in his spirit and to us in his words. For if we contend that those about whom it is not recorded whether or not they were baptized have left this life without baptism, we impugn the very apostles since, aside from the Apostle Paul, we do not know when they were baptized. But if we can deduce through what the Lord said to St. Peter, "He who has washed has no need of washing," that the disciples were baptized, what of the others about whom we read nothing of the sort—Barnabas, Timothy, Titus, Silas, Philemon, the very evangelists themselves Mark and Luke, and innumerable others? Far be it from us to doubt that they were baptized, though we do not read about it.

As for Dinocrates, he was a boy of seven, the age at which boys when they are baptized recite the creed and answer the questions for themselves. I do not know why it seems impossible to you that

he could have been recalled, though baptized, to the sacrileges of
pagan worship by his unbelieving father and was for this reason
undergoing the punishment from which he was freed by the prayers
of his sister. For you have not read either that he was never a Christian or that he died a catechumen. Besides, this account is not in
the canonical writings, from which, on this sort of question, the
evidence should always be cited.

13. Do not believe or say or teach that "those whom the Lord
has predestined to baptism can be snatched from their predestined
end and die before that which the Almighty has predestined can be
accomplished in them," if you wish to be a Catholic. For [on your
assumption] some power [acting] against the power of God is here
given to chance events which burst in to prevent what He predestined from taking place. I need not elaborate on how this error
would swallow up its perpetrator in a great abyss of impiety, since
a brief word suffices to warn a prudent man who is ready to be
corrected. But your words are as follows: "I would say that an opinion of this sort should be held regarding infants who, though predestined to baptism in their present life, before they are reborn in
Christ are prevented by death." Do you mean by this that those
predestined to baptism in this present life, before they attain it, are
prevented by death, and so God predestined what He foreknew
would not happen or else did not know that this would not happen?
So either His predestination is frustrated or His foreknowledge is
mistaken? You see how much could be said on this point unless I
should hold to what I said a little earlier, that I would warn you
briefly.

14. Do not believe or say or teach if you wish to be a Catholic:
"It is written concerning infants who, before they are reborn in
Christ, are prevented by death: 'He was snatched away lest wickedness pervert his understanding or falsehood deceive his soul. Because of this He hastened to lead him out of the midst of iniquity
. . . for his soul was pleasing to God.' And 'perfected in a short time,
he fulfilled a long time.'" For this [verse] does not apply at all to
those [who die unbaptized] but rather to those who, though baptized and leading a pious life, are not allowed to live here long, [and
are thus] perfected not by years but by the grace of wisdom. But
your error in taking this as a saying about infants who die before
they are baptized does intolerable wrong to that most holy washing
if it allows a little child who could be baptized before he is "snatched
away" to be snatched away first for this reason: "lest wickedness

pervert his understanding or falsehood deceive his soul," as though the wickedness and falsehood by which he is perverted and deceived lay in baptism itself, if he were snatched away before it. Finally [your interpretation would lead to the conclusion that] since his soul was pleasing to God, [God] hastened to remove him from the midst of iniquity; that God would not delay even a little in order to fulfill in him what He had predestined, but preferred to act against His predestination, as though He hastened for fear that what had pleased Him in the unbaptized person might be wiped out in baptism, as if a child that is going to die should perish at the very place to which one must run with him lest he perish!

Who, therefore, could believe that these words written in the Book of Wisdom were spoken concerning infants who die without baptism? Who could say, write, or proclaim so if he thinks about them as he ought?

15. Do not believe or say or teach that "there are some mansions, which the Lord said were in His Father's house, that are outside the kingdom of God," if you wish to be a Catholic. For He did not say, "With my Father there are many mansions" as you have quoted this text (and even if He had said that, one could not have understood it otherwise than "in the house of my Father"), but He plainly said, "In the house of my Father there are many mansions." Who then would dare to separate some parts of God's house from God's kingdom so that, when earthly kings are seen to rule not only in their own houses, not only in their own countries, but even far and wide across the sea, the king who made heaven and earth is not even said to reign over His whole house?

16. But perhaps you would object that all things do in fact belong to the kingdom of God since he rules in the heavens, in the earth, in the deep places, in paradise, in the abyss. For where does He not reign whose power is supreme everywhere? But [you would maintain] that the kingdom of Heaven is one thing, which one cannot attain except by washing in the baptism of regeneration, because of the Lord's true and fixed decree; but that the kingdom of earth and of the other parts of creation is something else, where there can be some mansions of the house of God belonging, if you will, to the kingdom of God, not, however, to the kingdom of heaven (where the kingdom of God is more excellent and blessed). Thus on the one hand, no regions or mansions of God's house would be crudely separated from the kingdom of God; but on the other hand, not all [the dwellings] would be prepared for inhabitants

within the kingdom of heaven. Yet they could dwell happily in those which are not in the kingdom of heaven which God wishes to give them, though they are not baptized, the result being that they are in the kingdom of God, although since they are not baptized, they cannot be in the kingdom of heaven.

17. Those who assert this indeed seem to themselves to be saying something [reasonable] because they do not attend properly to the Scriptures and do not understand how "kingdom of God" is meant when we pray "Thy kingdom come." What we call "the kingdom of God" is where His whole faithful family will rule with Him in eternal blessedness; for even now He surely reigns, in accordance with the power He has over everything. What is it, then, that we pray may come unless it is that we should be found worthy to reign with Him? Yet even those who will burn in the punishment of eternal fire will be under His power. But should we for that reason say that even those will be in the kingdom of God? Surely it is one thing to be honored with the rewards of the kingdom of God and quite another to be restrained by the laws of the kingdom of God. However, hear the Lord Himself so it may be absolutely clear to you that there is not a kingdom of heaven to be divided up among the baptized and other parts of the kingdom of God to be given to the unbaptized, as it seems to you. He does not say, "Unless one is born again of water and the Spirit, he cannot enter into the kingdom of *heaven*," but He says, ". . . he cannot enter into the kingdom of God." For these are His words to Nicodemus on this subject: "Truly, truly, I say to you, unless one is born anew, he cannot see the kingdom of God." Note that He does not say here "kingdom of heaven" but "of God." And when Nicodemus had answered and said, "How can a man be born when he is old? Can he enter a second time into his mother's womb and be born?" the Lord, repeating the same statement even more plainly and openly said: "Truly, truly I say to you, unless one is born again of water and the Spirit he cannot enter into the kingdom of God." Note that here too He does not say "kingdom of heaven" but "kingdom of God." Now that which He had said, [viz.] "unless one is born anew," He explained by saying "unless one is born again of water and the Spirit." And what He had said, [viz.] "cannot see," He explained by saying "cannot enter." But His designation "kingdom of God" He did not repeat by another name. So there is now no need to inquire or discuss whether "kingdom of God" and "kingdom of heaven" should be understood any differently or whether it is one thing called by two names; it is enough

that he who has not been cleansed by the washing of regeneration cannot enter the kingdom of God. I think you understand by now how far from the truth it is to separate some mansions set up in the house of God from the kingdom of God. As for your opinion that some who are not even born again of water and the Spirit will dwell in some mansions (which the Lord said were many) in the home of His Father, I advise you, if you allow me, not to delay in correcting [your idea], that you may hold the Catholic faith.

18. Do not believe or say or teach that "the sacrifice of Christians must be offered on behalf of those who have departed from the body unbaptized," if you wish to be a Catholic. For you do not prove that even that sacrifice of the Jews which you cited from the Book of Maccabees was offered on behalf of those who departed from the body uncircumcised. In presenting such a novel opinion as this, that goes against the authority and discipline of the whole Church, you have even used very insolent language, saying: "It is my judgment that continuous oblations and constant sacrifices should surely be offered on behalf of these [unbaptized souls] by the holy priests." So you, a layman, neither submit yourself to the authority of the priests of God for instruction, nor do you even associate with them on the same level in your inquiry, but you put yourself above them by stating your judgment. Cease from that, my son. Not thus does one walk in the way which Christ humbly taught that He was; no one enters through His narrow door with such swollen pride as this.

19. Do not believe or say or teach that "some of those who have passed over from this life without the baptism of Christ do not go for the present into the kingdom of heaven but into paradise, but afterwards in the resurrection of the dead they too shall attain the blessedness of the kingdom of heaven," if you wish to be a Catholic. Not even the Pelagian heresy, which holds that infants do not contract original sin, has dared to grant them this. Although as a Catholic you confess that men are born in sin, nevertheless you assert by some novel perversity of opinion, that they are saved without baptism, absolved from the sin with which they are born, and ushered into the kingdom of heaven. You do not consider how much less sensible you are than Pelagius on this question. He at least greatly fears the Lord's decree that the unbaptized are not permitted to enter the kingdom of heaven and does not dare to assign little ones there though he believes them to be free from any sin. But you have so little respect for what is written, [viz.] "unless one is

born again of water and the Spirit he cannot enter into the kingdom of God," that (even apart from the error of daring to separate paradise from the kingdom of God) you do not hesitate to promise both absolution from their guilt and the kingdom of heaven besides to some who die without baptism, though as a Catholic you acknowledge that they are born guilty. It is as if by bringing up arguments against Pelagius on original sin [you think] you can thereby be a true Catholic even if, by tearing down His decree concerning baptism, you become a new heretic against the Lord. Not thus, my beloved, do we wish you to be the victor over heretics, by vanquishing error with error, and worse yet, a smaller error with a greater one. For you say, "If by chance anyone should object to the temporary assignment of the souls of the thief or Dinocrates to paradise—for the prize of the kingdom of heaven still waits for them in the resurrection although that principal saying [of the Lord] counts against it,/1/ [viz.] 'unless one is born again of water and the Spirit, he cannot enter into the kingdom'—nevertheless let him have my ungrudging assent if only he magnifies both the result and the working out [effectum et affectum] of the divine mercy and foreknowledge." These are your words, and you confess here that you agree with one who says that paradise is assigned temporarily to some who are not baptized so that there is left to them in the resurrection the prize of the kingdom of heaven, contrary to the principal saying by which it is determined that no one shall enter that kingdom unless he is born again of water and the Holy Spirit. Pelagius, fearing to violate this principal saying, did not even believe that those whom he did not think guilty would enter the kingdom of heaven without baptism. You, however, confess that even infants are guilty of original sin, but nevertheless you absolve them without the washing of regeneration, send them to paradise, and afterwards even allow them to enter the kingdom of heaven.

20. These [errors] and any others like them (if you are able to find more by taking time and looking more carefully) correct without delay if you bear a Catholic mind; that is, if you were telling the truth before when you wrote that you yourself are not firmly convinced that what you say can be proved, that you are always careful not to leap to the defense of even your own opinions if they are shown to be unlikely, and that you are heartily ready to pursue better and truer [opinions] if yours are condemned. Only prove, my beloved, that you did not say this falsely. Then the Catholic Church may rejoice in your natural talent not only because it is

inventive but because it is circumspect, pious, and modest, and not be inflamed by heretical madness because of your quarrelsome tenacity. Now is the time to show how sincere your heart was when you spoke those good words I have just reminded you of, for you immediately added, "for as it is characteristic of the best purpose and praiseworthy resolve to be converted readily to more perfect truths, so it is the mark of a perverse and stubborn judgment to refuse to be quickly conformed to the path of reason." Well then, show your best purpose and praiseworthy resolve and your readiness to convert to more perfect truths, and do not show such a perverse and stubborn judgment that you refuse to be conformed to the path of reason. If you expressed yourself honestly, if you did not just make sounds with your lips but genuinely felt this way in your heart, you have shown your hatred of any delay in such a good thing as your correction. Indeed you found it too little to say that it was "the mark of a perverse and stubborn judgment to refuse to be conformed to the path of reason" unless you added "quickly." By this you intended to show how accursed he must be who never accomplishes this good action, when even he who accomplishes it too slowly seemed to you worthy of such harsh criticism that he deserved to be called [a man] "of perverse and stubborn judgment." Therefore, listen to yourself and make use especially and principally of the fruits of your own eloquence so that you may conform yourself with a serious mind to the path of reason more quickly than you deviated from it in a manner quite unlearned and ill-considered due to the instability of youth.

21. It would take too long to draw out and discuss everything in your books, or rather in yourself, that I wish to see corrected and to give even a short argument concerning each single point that needs correction. Nevertheless, do not despise yourself or think that your talent and eloquence are of little value. Nor do I consider that your acquaintance with sacred Scripture is negligible; but your learning is less than is appropriate to such great talent and labor. And so I neither wish you to grow vain by crediting yourself with more than you should, nor do I want you to become paralyzed by dejection and despair. If only I could read your writings with you and show you in conversation rather than in writing what should be corrected! This business could be accomplished far more easily by discussion between us than by letters. If [everything] were to be written down, it would take many volumes. But these main points, which I wanted to hold to a definite number, I warn you urgently

to correct without delay and to banish absolutely from your faith and public discourse, so that whatever natural ability you have in debate, you may employ that gift of God usefully for the edification, not the destruction, of sound and healthy doctrine.

22. These are your points that I have discussed as well as I was able, but I will run through them again briefly:

1) that God did not make the soul from nothing but from Himself.
2) that through infinite time and always God gives souls, even as He who gives always exists.
3) that the soul, through [being incarnated in] flesh lost some merit which it had before [being incarnated in] flesh.
4) that the soul through flesh is restored to its primal state and is reborn through that same flesh by which it deserved to be corrupted.
5) that the soul deserved to be a sinner before any sin.
6) that infants who die before they can be baptized can obtain forgiveness of their original sin.
7) that those whom the Lord has predestined to baptism can be snatched from their predestined end and die before that which the Almighty has predestined can be accomplished in them.
8) that the passage "He was snatched away lest wickedness pervert his understanding," and the rest of that sentence which we read in the Book of Wisdom, is written concerning infants who die before they are reborn in Christ.
9) that there are some mansions, which the Lord said were in His Father's house, that are outside of the kingdom of God.
10) that the sacrifice of Christians must be offered on behalf of those who have departed from the body unbaptized.
11) that some of those who have passed over from this life without the baptism of Christ do not go for the present into the kingdom [of heaven] but into paradise, but afterwards in the resurrection of the dead they too shall attain the blessedness of the kingdom of heaven.

23. For the present, do not delay to root out at once these eleven points which contain much that is plainly erroneous and opposed to the Catholic faith, and cast them away from your mind, from your speech, from your pen, if you want us to rejoice that you have not only crossed over to the altars of the Catholics but that you are truly a Catholic. For these points, if stubbornly defended one by one, can spawn as many heresies as the number of opinions. Consider, therefore, how dreadful it would be for the heresies which would be individually damnable in individual men to be

found all in one man. However, if you do not fight contentiously to defend them but rather battle to overcome them by faithful words and writings, you will deserve more praise in censuring yourself than in reproving any other person with correct reasoning, and you will deserve more admiration in correcting [your false opinions] than if you had never held to them. May the Lord be present to your mind and flood your spirit by His Spirit with such willing humility, such light of truth, sweetness of love, and peaceful piety, that you would rather be victor over your own mind in truth than over any adversary in falsehood. God forbid that you should believe you have fallen away from the Catholic faith by holding these opinions (although they are opposed to the Catholic faith) if before God, whose eye is not deceived by any heart, you recognize that you spoke truly [when you said] that you are not firmly convinced that what you say can be proved and that you are always careful not to defend even your own opinions if they are shown to be unlikely, because you are heartily ready to pursue better and truer [opinions] if yours are condemned. Indeed a mind, even when its formulations are uncatholic through ignorance, is Catholic by the very premeditation of and readiness for amendment. But let this be enough for this volume, where the reader may rest a bit, that his attention may be renewed at the introduction of what follows.

NOTE to Appendix A

/1/   Note: *principalis* has a double meaning: "principal" but also "pertaining to the Prince," i.e., a Dominical saying.

APPENDIX B

Book IV, 9–10 and 15–16 of
De Natura et Origine Animae

9. Just observe how while we exist, while we live, while we
know we are alive, while we are certain that we remember and
think and will, we, who boast that we are the great experts on our
own nature, are altogether ignorant of the powers of our memory
and thought and will. A certain friend of mine with whom I grew
up, Simplicius by name, had an excellent and remarkable memory.
[Once] when we asked him what verses Vergil had written next to
the last in all his books, he answered at once, quickly and from
memory. Then we asked him the verses that came before those; he
recited them. So we began to think that he could recite the whole
of Vergil backwards. We asked him to do it from whatever passage
we wished; he did it. Likewise, we asked him to do [the same thing]
with prose from any oration of Cicero which he knew by heart. He
responded with the preceding passages, as far as we wanted. When
we marveled, he vowed in God's name that he had not known he
could do this before our experiment. Thus, as far as his memory
was concerned, his mind came to know itself at that moment; indeed whenever it came to know itself, it could only do so through
trial and experiment. And yet before he tried this, surely he was
the same person. Why then was he ignorant of his own self?

10. Often we assume that we will remember something, and
because we think this, we do not write it down. But afterwards
when we want to recall it to mind we cannot, and we regret that we
thought it would come to us and that we did not get it down in
writing so that it would not escape. But suddenly it comes back to
us when we are not looking for it. Does that mean we were not
ourselves when we were thinking of it? Nevertheless, we are not
what we were when we were unable to think of it. How is it then

that in some way we are abstracted from and denied to ourselves and subsequently restored somehow and given back to ourselves? [It is] as though we were different people or in some other place when we seek but do not find what we have stored in our memory; and we are unable to return to ourselves, as though we were in another place, and then we return to ourselves when we have found it. For where should we seek other than within ourselves? Or what should we seek if not ourselves (as if we were not in ourselves and had departed from ourselves to some other place)? Do you not mark and stand awestruck before such a profound [mystery]? And what is this, other than our own nature, not as it once was but as it is now? You see that there are more questions than answers.

Often when a question has been proposed to me, I have thought that I would find a solution if I thought about it. I thought about it and could not [solve it]; [but] often I have not thought about it and solved it nevertheless. And so in the end the powers of my own intelligence are unknown to me and, I suspect, [yours are] to you too.

******

15. But you are mistaken here too. For the divine testimonies which you wished to apply to the resolution of this problem do not [in fact] solve it. What they prove is something else (without which, to be sure, we could not live a pious life), viz., that we hold God to be the giver, creator, and shaper of our souls. But *how* He does this—whether by breathing them into us new or by deriving them from the parents—[the Scripture texts] do not tell us except in the case of that one [soul] which He gave to the first human being. Read carefully what I wrote to our brother Renatus, servant of God; for since I demonstrated this to him there, it is not necessary for me to write it down here too. However, you would like me to give a clear definition, as you did yourself, so that I might get entangled in the same difficulties as you have yourself. Thus entangled, you have made so many serious assertions against the Catholic faith that if only you would recollect and reconsider them with faith and humility, you would see at once how profitable it would have been for you if you had recognized your own ignorance [*scisses nescire quod nescis*], and how greatly it would still profit you if you knew now. For if understanding [*intelligentia*] pleases you in human nature (and if we lacked it, we should truly be no different from beasts with respect to our souls), [then] understand what you do not understand so that you will not totally lack understanding, and do

not despise the person who, in order to get a true understanding of what he does not understand, understands that he does not understand it. But as for the reason why it is said in the sacred Psalm: "Although man was held in honor, he did not understand; he is like the cattle and can be compared to them," read and understand so that you may avoid this opprobrium yourself in all humility rather than hurl it proudly at someone else. For this passage is said about those who regard this life as the only one, living according to the flesh and hoping for nothing after death, like cattle. [It does] not [concern] those who do not deny that they know what they know and who confess that they do not know what they do not know and who understand their own weakness more thoroughly than they trust their own strength.

16. Therefore, my son, do not let my old man's timidity displease your youthful presumption. For my part, if I find that I am unable to discover, either from God or from a human spiritual teacher, what we are seeking concerning the origin of souls, I am more ready to defend God's right to withhold from us the knowledge of this (as of many other things) than to make some rash assertion that either is so obscure that I cannot understand it myself, let alone produce understanding in others, or that is undoubtedly useful to the heretics. They try to persuade [us] that the souls of infants are pure and free from any fault for the apparent reason that the same fault would [otherwise] reflect on or go back to God as its Author, because He compelled innocent souls, though He foreknew that the washing of regeneration would not come to their aid, to become sinners by assigning them to sinful flesh without [the prospect of] baptismal grace intervening by which they would be freed from eternal damnation. For it is true that innumerable infants' souls pass out of their bodies before they are baptized. But God forbid that out of a desire to dilute this [fact] I should say what you yourself have said, that 'the soul deserved to be corrupted through flesh and become a sinner,' though it had no sin before for which it might be said to have deserved this. Nor [would I say, as you have said,] that 'even without baptism original sins are remitted and that even the kingdom of heaven is finally bestowed on those who are not baptized.' If I were not afraid to express these [ideas] and [others] like them [which are] poisonous to the faith, perhaps I would not be afraid to give a definite opinion on this question. But then how much better not to dispute and affirm point by point what I do

not know about the soul but simply to hold to what I see the apostle has taught very plainly: that from one man all men who are born from Adam pass into condemnation unless they are born again in Christ in the way that He instituted for their rebirth before their physical death; these He has predestined to eternal life as the most merciful bestower of grace; but to those whom He has predestined to eternal death, He is the most just awarder of punishment, not only for those sins which they add voluntarily but even for original sin, if, being infants, they add nothing to it.

This is my definite opinion on this question; so the hidden works of God preserve their secret and my faith remains secure.

BIBLIOGRAPHY

Reference and Primary Sources

Andresen, Carl. *Bibliographia Augustiniana.* 2nd revised ed. Darmstadt: Wissenschaftliche Buchgesellschaft, 1973.

Aristotle. *Rhetoric.* Trans. W. Rhys Roberts. New York: Random House (Modern Library), 1954.

Augustine, Aurelius. *De Beata Vita.* PL 32, cols. 959–976; CSEL 63, pp. 89–116; CCL 29, pp. 65–85; FOC 1.

———. *De Catechizandis Rudibus.* PL 40, cols. 309–348; CCL 46, pp. 121–178.

The First Catechetical Instruction. Trans. Joseph Christopher. ACW 2. New York: Newman Press, 1946.

———. *De Civitate Dei.* PL 41, cols. 13–804; CSEL 40; CCL 47–48.

City of God. Trans. Henry Bettenson. New York: Penguin Books, 1972.

City of God Against the Pagans. Trans. George McCracken. 7 vols. Loeb Classical Library. Cambridge: Harvard University Press, 1957–72.

———. *Confessiones.* PL 32, cols. 659–868; CSEL 33; CCL 27.

The Confessions of St. Augustine. Trans. John K. Ryan. New York: Image Books, 1960.

St. Augustine's Confessions. Trans. W. Watts, rev. W. H. D. Rouse. 2 vols. Loeb Classical Library. New York: Macmillan, 1912.

———. *De Doctrina Christiana.* PL 34, cols. 15–122; CSEL 80, pp. 3–169; CCL 32, pp. 1–167.

On Christian Doctrine. Trans. D. W. Robertson. LLA 80. Indianapolis: Bobbs-Merrill, 1958.

De doctrina christiana liber quartus: A Commentary with a Revised Text, Introduction, and Translation. Trans. Sr. Thérèse Sullivan. Patristic Studies 23. Washington, D.C.: Catholic University of America Press, 1930.

———. *Epistulae.* PL 33; CSEL 34 (*Ep.* 1–123), 44–45 (*Ep.* 124–184a), 57 (*Ep.* 185–270); FOC 12, 18, 20, 30, 32.

———. *De Genesi ad Litteram.* PL 34, cols. 245–486; CSEL 28:1, pp. 3–435.

    La Génèse au sens littéral, livres I-XII. Trans. P. Agaësse et A. Solignac. BA, Oeuvres de St. Augustin, vols. 48–49. Paris: Desclée de Brouwer, 1972.

    The Literal Meaning of Genesis. Trans. John H. Taylor. ACW 41. New York: Newman Press, 1982.

    Über den Wortlaut der Genesis. 2 vols. Trans. Carl Johan Perl. Munich: Schöningh, 1964.

———. *De Magistro.* PL 32, cols. 1193–1220; CSEL 77, pp. 3–57; CCL 29, pp. 157–203.

    Concerning the Teacher and On the Immortality of the Soul. Trans. George G. Leckie. New York: Appleton-Century-Crofts, 1938.

    The Greatness of the Soul, The Teacher. Trans. Joseph Colleran. ACW 9. New York: Newman Press, 1950.

———. *De Natura et Origine Animae.* PL 44, cols. 475–548; CSEL 60, pp. 303–419.

    De natura et origine animae libri IV. Trans. J. Plagnieux and F. J. Thonnard. BA, Oeuvres de St. Augustin, vol. 22, *La crise Pélagienne* II. Paris: Desclée de Brouwer, 1975.

    Natur und Ursprung der Seele. Trans. Anton Fingerle, A. Maxsein, D. Morick. vol. 3 of Sankt Augustinus, der Lehrer der Gnade: Schriften gegen die Pelagianer. Würzburg: Augustinus-Verlag, 1977.

    On the Soul and Its Origin. Trans. Peter Holmes. PNF, 1st series, vol. 5: Writings Against the Pelagians. 1887; rpt. Grand Rapids: Eerdmans, 1971.

———. *Retractationes.* PL 32, cols. 583–658.

    The Retractations. Trans. Mary Inez Bogan. ACW 60. New York: Newman Press, 1968.

———. *Soliloquiorum libri II.* PL 32, cols 869–904; PNF, 1st series, vol. 7, pp. 537–560.

———. *De Trinitate.* PL 42, cols. 819–1098; CCL 50–50A.

    The Trinity in *Augustine: Later Works.* Trans. John Burnaby. Library of Christian Classics, vol. 8. Philadelphia: Westminster, 1960.

Blaise, Albert. *Dictionnaire latin-français des auteurs chrétiens.* Turnhout, Belgium: Éditions Brepols, 1954.

———. *Manuel du latin chrétien.* Strasbourg: Le Latin Chrétien, 1955.

The Catholic Encyclopedia, 1907 ed.

Cicero. *Brutus.* Trans. G. L. Hendrickson. Loeb Classical Library. Cambridge: Harvard University Press, 1939.

———. *de Oratore.* Trans. E. W. Sutton and H. Rackham. Loeb Classical Library. Cambridge: Harvard University Press, 1957.

———. *Orator.* Trans. H. M. Hubbell. Loeb Classical Library. Cambridge: Harvard University Press, 1939.

———. *Partitiones Oratoriae.* Trans. H. Rackham. Loeb Classical Library. Cambridge: Harvard University Press, 1958.

———. *Tusculan Disputations.* Trans. J. E. King. Loeb Classical Library. Cambridge: Harvard University Press, 1945.

Cyprian. *Treatises.* Trans. and ed. by Roy J. Deferrari. FOC 36. Washington, D.C.: Catholic University of America Press, 1958.

Dictionnaire de théologie catholique, 1909 ed.

Macrobius. *Commentary on the Dream of Scipio.* Trans., intro., and notes by Wm. Harris Stahl. Records of Civilization. New York: Columbia University Press, 1952.

Origen. *On First Principles.* Trans. G. W. Butterworth. New York: Harper Torchbooks, 1966.

Orosius. *Consultatio Commonitorium Orosii ad Augustinum et ad Orosium contra Priscillianistas et Origenistas, liber I.* PL 42, cols. 666–678.

———. *The Seven Books of History against the Pagans.* Trans. Roy J. Deferrari. FOC 50. Washington, D.C.: Catholic University of America Press, 1964.

Paulys Real-Encyclopädie der classischen Altertumswissenschaft. Stuttgart: Metzler, 1940.

Perpetua, The Passion of St. Ed. J. Armitage Robinson. Texts and Studies, 1:2. Cambridge: Cambridge University Press, 1891.

Plato. *The Collected Dialogues of Plato.* Ed. E. Hamilton and H. Cairns. Bollingen Series, 71. New York: Pantheon Books, 1963.

Tertullian. *Quinti Florentii Tertulliani de anima.* Trans. and comm. J. H. Waszink. Amsterdam: Meulenhoff, 1947.

————. *A Treatise on the Soul*. Trans. S. Thelwall. ANF 3. Buffalo: The Christian Literature Publishing Co., 1887, pp. 181–235.

Van Bavel, Tarsicius. *Répertoire bibliographique de St. Augustin 1950–1960*. The Hague: Nijhoff, 1968.

Xenophon. *Memorabilia*. Trans. Marchant. Loeb Classical Library. London: Heinemann, 1923.

Secondary Sources

Aland, Kurt. *Did the Early Church Baptize Infants?* Trans. G. R. Beasley-Murray. Philadelphia: Westminster, 1963.

Armstong, A. H. and R. A. Markus. *Christian Faith and Greek Philosophy*. London: Darton, Longman & Todd, 1960.

Auerbach, Erich. *Literary Language and Its Public in Late Latin Antiquity and in the Middle Ages*. Trans. Ralph Manheim. Bollingen Series, 74. New York: Pantheon Books, 1965.

Ayers, R. H. *Language, Logic, and Reason in the Church Fathers*. Hildesheim: George Olms, 1979.

Baldwin, Charles Sears. *Medieval Rhetoric and Poetic*. New York: Macmillan, 1928.

Barnes, Timothy David. *Tertullian: A Historical and Literary Study*. Oxford: Clarendon Press, 1971.

Barry, Sr. M. Inviolata. *St. Augustine the Orator: A Study of the Rhetorical Qualities of St. Augustine's 'Sermones ad Populum'*. Patristic Studies, No. 6. Washington: Catholic University of America, 1924.

Bonaiuti, Ernesto. "The Genesis of St. Augustine's Idea of Original Sin." *Harvard Theological Review*, 10 (1917), pp. 159–175.

Bonner, Gerald. "Augustine's Visit to Caesarea in 418." In *Studies in Church History*, vol. 1. Ed. C. W. Dugmore and Charles Duggan. London: Nelson, 1964, pp. 104–113.

Bouyer, Louis. *Woman and Man with God*. Trans. Fr. A. V. Littledale. London: Darton, Longman, & Todd, 1960.

Brown, Peter. *Augustine of Hippo*. Berkeley: University of California Press, 1967.

————. *The World of Late Antiquity*. London: Thames & Hudson, 1971.

Burke, Kenneth. *The Rhetoric of Religion*. Berkeley: University of California Press, 1970.

Burnaby, John. *Amor Dei.* London: Hodder and Stoughton, 1938; rpt. 1947.

Chadwick, Henry. *Priscillian of Avila. The Occult and the Charismatic in the Early Church.* Oxford: Clarendon, 1976.

Clark, Donald Lemen. *Rhetoric in Greco-Roman Education.* New York: Columbia University Press, 1957.

Courcelle, Pierre. *"Connais-toi toi-même" de Socrate à St. Bernard,* 3 vols. Paris: Études augustiniennes, 1974.

————. *Late Latin Writers and Their Greek Sources.* Trans. Harry E. Wedeck. Cambridge: Harvard University Press, 1969.

————. *Recherches sur les "Confessions" de St. Augustin.* 2nd ed. Paris: E. de Boccard, 1968.

Courtes, J. "St. Augustin et la médecine." *Augustinus Magister,* vol. 1. Paris: Études augustiniennes, 1954–55, pp. 43–51.

de Veer, Albert C. Introduction to *De natura et origine animae libri IV,* BA, Oeuvres de St. Augustin, vol. 22, *La Crise Pélagienne* II. Paris: Desclée de Brouwer, 1975.

————. "Origines de *De natura et origine animae* de St. Augustin." *REA* 19:1–2 (1973), pp. 121–157.

Didier, J.-Ch. *Faut-il baptiser les enfants? La réponse de la tradition.* Paris: Éditions du Cerf, 1967.

Dieter, Otto and Wm. Kurth. "The *De Rhetorica* of Aurelius Augustine." *Speech Monographs,* 35 (1968), pp. 90–108.

Dodds, E. R. *Pagan and Christian in an Age of Anxiety.* Cambridge: Cambridge University Press, 1965.

du Roy, Olivier. *L'intelligence de la foi en la trinité selon St. Augustin.* Paris: Études augustiniennes, 1966.

Ellspermann, Gerard L. *The Attitude of the Early Christian Latin Writers Toward Pagan Literature and Learning.* Patristic Studies, No. 82. Washington: Catholic University of America Press, 1949.

Eskridge, James Burnette. *The Influence of Cicero upon Augustine in the Development of his Oratorical Theory for the Training of the Ecclesiastical Orator.* Dissertation University of Chicago, n.d. Menasha, WI: Collegiate Press, 1912.

Fairweather, E. R. "St. Augustine's Interpretation of Infant Baptism." *Augustinus Magister,* vol. II. Paris: Études augustiniennes, 1954, pp. 897-903.

Ferguson, John. "Aspects of Early Christianity in North Africa." In *Africa in Classical Antiquity.* Ed. L. Thompson and J. Ferguson. Ibadan: Ibadan University Press, 1969.

————. *Pelagius*. Cambridge: W. Heffer, 1956.

Ferraz, M. *De la psychologie de St. Augustin*. Paris: Thorin, 1869.

Finaert, Joseph. *L'Évolution littéraire de St. Augustin*. Paris: Société des études latines, 1939.

————. *Saint Augustin rhéteur*. Paris: Société des études latines, 1939.

Fingerle, Anton, A. Maxsein, and D. Morick (trans., notes). *Natur und Ursprung der Seele*, vol. 3 of *Sankt Augustinus, der Lehrer der Gnade: Schriften gegen die Pelagianer*. Würzburg: Augustinus-Verlag, 1977.

Fondation Hardt pour l'étude de l'antiquité classique. *Christianisme et formes littéraires de l'antiquité tardive en Occident*, vol. 23. Geneva: Vandoeuvres, 1976.

Fortin, Ernest. "Augustine and the Problem of Christian Rhetoric." *Augustinian Studies*, 5 (1974), pp. 85–100.

————. *Christianisme et culture philosophique au cinquième siècle, la querelle de l'âme humaine en Occident*. Paris: Études augustiniennes, 1959.

Fredriksen, Paula Lee. "Augustine's Early Interpretation of Paul, 386–398." Dissertation. Princeton, 1979.

Frend, W. H. C. *The Donatist Church*. Oxford: Clarendon, 1952.

Friedländer, Paul. *Plato*. Trans. Hans Meyerhoff. 2nd ed. 1969. Princeton: Princeton University Press, Bollingen Foundation, 1958.

Geffcken, J. *Sokrates und das alte Christentum*. Heidelberg: Winters, 1908.

Geiger, James A. *The Origin of the Soul: An Augustinian Dilemma*. Dissertation. Rome: Angelicum, 1957.

Gilson, Etienne. *The Christian Philosophy of St. Augustine*. Trans. L. E. M. Lynch. New York: Random House, 1960.

Grassi, Ernesto. "Can Rhetoric Provide a New Basis for Philosophizing? The Humanist Tradition." *Philosophy and Rhetoric*, 11:1 (1978), pp. 1–17 and 11:2 (1978), pp. 75–95.

————. *Rhetoric as Philosophy: The Humanist Tradition*. University Park & London: Pennsylvania State University Press, 1980.

Grimaldi, William. M. A. *Studies in the Philosophy of Aristotle's Rhetoric*. Wiesbaden: Steiner, 1972.

Hagendahl, Harald. *Augustine and the Latin Classics*. Göteborg: Statens Humanistiska Forskningsråd, 1967.

Harnack, Adolf. *Sokrates und die alte Kirche*. Berlin: Königlichen Friedrich-Wilhelms-Universität, 1900.

Heinzelmann, W. "Über Augustins Lehre vom Wesen and Ursprung der menschlichen Seele." Halberstadt: Jahresbericht über das Königliche Domgymnasium, 1868.

Henry, Margaret Young. *The Relation of Dogmatism and Scepticism in the Philosophical Treatises of Cicero*. Dissertation. Columbia, 1925. Geneva, NY: W. F. Humphrey, 1925.

Henry, Paul. *Plotin et l'Occident*. Louvain: Spicilegium Sacrum Lovaniense bureaux, 1934.

Ijsseling, Samuel. *Rhetoric and Philosophy in Conflict*. The Hague: Nijhoff, 1976.

Ivánka, Endre von. *Plato Christianus. Übernahme und Umgestaltung des Platonismus durch die Väter*. Einsiedeln: Johannes Verlag, 1964.

Jeremias, Joachim. *Infant Baptism in the First Four Centuries*. Trans. D. Cairns. Philadelphia: Westminster Press, 1960.

————. *The Origins of Infant Baptism*. Trans. D. Barton. Naperville, IN: A. R. Allenson, 1963.

Johnson, W. R. "Isocrates Flowering: The Rhetoric of Augustine." *Philosophy and Rhetoric*, 9:4 (1976), pp. 217–231.

Jones, A. H. M. "Were Ancient Heresies National or Social Movements in Disguise?" *Journal of Theological Studies*, New Series, vol. X, part 2 (1959), pp. 280–297.

Karpp, Heinrich. *Probleme altchristlicher Anthropologie: Biblische Anthropologie und philosophische Psychologie bei den Kirchenvätern des dritten Jahrhunderts*. Beiträge zur Förderung Christlicher Theologie, Band 44, Heft 3. Gütersloh: C. Bertelsmann Verlag, 1950.

Kelly, Louis G. "St. Augustine and Saussurean Linguistics." *Augustinian Studies* 6 (1975), pp. 45–64.

Kennedy, George. *The Art of Persuasion in Greece*. Princeton: Princeton University Press, 1963.

————. *Classical Rhetoric and Its Christian and Secular Tradition from Ancient to Modern Times*. Chapel Hill: University of North Carolina Press, 1980.

Kennedy, H. A. A. *Philo's Contribution to Religion*. London: Hodder & Stoughton, 1919.

Keseling, Paul. "Augustin und Quintilian." *Augustinus Magister*, vol. I. Paris: Études augustiniennes, 1954, pp. 201–204.

Kevane, E. "Augustine and Isocrates." *American Ecclesiastical Review* 149 (1963), pp. 301–321.

Knox, Bernard M. W. "Silent Reading in Antiquity." *Greek, Roman and Byzantine Studies*, 9:4 (1968), pp. 421–435.

Kunzle, Pius. *Das Verhältnis der Seele zu ihren Potenzen: Problemgeschichtliche Untersuchungen von Augustin bis und mit Thomas von Aquin.* Freiburg, Switzerland: Universitätsverlag, 1956.

LaCroix, Robert. *L'origine de l'âme humaine.* Québec: L'action catholique, 1945.

Laistner, Max L. W. *Christianity and Pagan Culture in the Later Roman Empire.* Ithaca, NY: Cornell University Press, 1951.

————. "The Christian Attitude to Pagan Literature." *History*, 20 (1935), pp. 49–54.

Lossky, Vladimir. "Les éléments de 'théologie négative' dans la pensée de saint Augustin." *Augustinus Magister*, vol. I. Paris: Études augustiniennes, 1954, pp. 575–581.

Markus, Robert, ed. *Augustine: A Collection of Critical Essays.* New York: Anchor Books, 1972.

————. *Christianity in the Roman World.* New York: Scribners, 1974.

————. *Saeculum: History and Society in the Theology of St. Augustine.* Cambridge: Cambridge University Press, 1970.

Marrou, Henri-Irénée. *A History of Education in Antiquity.* Trans. George Lamb. New York: Sheed & Ward, 1956.

————. *St. Augustin et la fin de la culture antique.* Paris: E. de Boccard, 1938.

Mazzeo, Joseph Anthony. "St. Augustine's Rhetoric of Silence." *Journal of the History of Ideas*, 23 (1962), pp. 175–196.

McNew, Louis D. "The Relation of Cicero's Rhetoric to Augustine." *Research Studies of the State College of Washington*, 25:1 (March, 1957),pp. 5–13.

Mohrmann, Christine. *Études sur le latin des chrétiens*, vol. IV. Rome: Edizioni di storia e letteratura, 1977.

Momigliano, Arnaldo, ed. *The Conflict Between Paganism and Christianity in the Fourth Century.* Oxford: Clarendon, 1963.

Monceaux, Paul. *Histoire littéraire de l'Afrique chrétienne depuis les origines jusqu'à l'invasion arabe.* 7 vols. Paris: E. Leroux, 1901–1923.

Murphy, James J., ed. *Medieval Eloquence: Studies in the Theory and Practice of Medieval Rhetoric.* Berkeley: University of California Press, 1978.

———. "The Metarhetoric of Plato, Augustine, and McLuhan: A Pointing Essay." *Philosophy and Rhetoric*, 4:4 (1971), pp. 201–214.

———. *Rhetoric in the Middle Ages: A History of Rhetorical Theory from St. Augustine to the Renaissance.* Berkeley: University of California Press, 1974.

———. "St. Augustine and the Debate about a Christian Rhetoric." *Quarterly Journal of Speech*, 46 (1960), pp. 400–410.

———. "St. Augustine and Rabanus Maurus: The Genesis of Medieval Rhetoric." *Western Speech*, 31 (1967), pp. 88–96.

———. *A Synoptic History of Classical Rhetoric.* New York: Random House, 1972.

Nash, Ronald H. *The Light of the Mind: St. Augustine's Theory of Knowledge.* Lexington: University of Kentucky Press, 1969.

Nock, Arthur Darby. *Conversion.* Oxford: Clarendon, 1933.

Nygren, Anders. *Agape and Eros.* Trans. A. G. Hebert. London: SPCK, 1932.

O'Connell, Robert. *Confessions: The Odyssey of Soul.* Cambridge: Belknap Press of Harvard University Press, 1969.

———. "Pre-existence in Augustine's Seventh Letter." REA 15 (1969), pp. 67–73.

———. *St. Augustine's Early Theory of Man, 386–391.* Cambridge: Belknap Press of Harvard University Press, 1968.

O'Connor, William P. *The Concept of the Human Soul According to St. Augustine.* Dissertation. Catholic University of America, 1921.

O'Daly, Gerald J. P. "Did Augustine Ever Believe in the Soul's Pre-existence?" *Augustinian Studies*, 5 (1974), pp. 227–235.

O'Meara, John J. *The Young Augustine.* London: Longmans, 1954.

Plagnieux, J., and F. J. Thonnard, trans. and notes to *De natura et origine animae libri IV*, BA, Oeuvres de St. Augustin, vol. 22, *La crise Pélagienne* II. Paris: Desclée de Brouwer, 1975.

Pontet, Maurice. *L'exégèse de St. Augustin prédicateur.* [Paris]: Aubier [1945].

Reynolds, Graham. *The Clausulae in the 'De Civitate Dei' of St. Augustine.* Patristic Studies, No. 7. Washington: Catholic University of America, 1924.

Rist, John M. *Eros and Psyche: Studies in Plato, Plotinus and Origen.* Toronto: University of Toronto Press, 1964.

———. *Plotinus: The Road to Reality.* Cambridge: Cambridge University Press, 1967.

Robinson, T. M. *Plato's Psychology.* Toronto: University of Toronto Press, 1970.

Ruether, Rosemary R. *Gregory of Nazianzus, Rhetor and Philosopher.* Oxford: Clarendon, 1969.

Sage, A. "Péché originel. Naissance d'un dogme." *REA* 13 (1967), pp. 211–248.

Semple. W. H. "Augustinus Rhetor." *Journal of Ecclesiastical History,* 1 (1950), pp. 135–150.

Sider, Robert Dick. *Ancient Rhetoric and the Art of Tertullian.* Oxford: Oxford University Press, 1971.

Solmsen, Friedrich. "The Aristotelian Tradition in Ancient Rhetoric." *American Journal of Philology,* 62 (1941), pp. 35–50.

———. Introduction to Aristotle's *Rhetoric* and *Poetics.* New York: Random House (Modern Library), 1954.

Somers, H. "Image de Dieu. Les sources de L'exégèse augustinienne." *REA* 7 (1961), pp. 105–125.

Spanneut, Michel. *Le stoïcisme des pères de l'église de Clément de Rome à Clément d'Alexandrie.* Paris: Éditions du Seuil, 1957.

Stead, G. C. "Divine Substance in Tertullian." *Journal of Theological Studies,* 14:1 (April, 1963), pp. 47–67.

Taylor, J. H. "St. Augustine and the *Hortensius* of Cicero." *Studies in Philology,* 60:3 (1963), pp. 487–498.

———. "Sancti Aurelii Augustini *de Genesi ad litteram* liber duo decimus." Dissertation. St. Louis University, 1948.

TeSelle, Eugene. *Augustine the Theologian.* New York: Herder & Herder, 1970.

Testard, Maurice. *Saint Augustin et Cicéron.* Paris: Études augustiniennes, 1958.

———. "Saint Augustin et Cicéron: à propos d'un ouvrage récent." *REA* 14 (1968), pp. 47–67.

Van Der Meer, F. *Augustine the Bishop.* Trans. Battershaw and Lamb. New York: Sheed & Ward, 1961.

Verbeke, G. *L'Évolution de la doctrine du pneuma du stoïcisme à St. Augustin.* Paris: Desclée du Brouwer, 1945.

Waszink, J. H. *Quinti Septimi Florentis Tertulliani De Anima.* Amsterdam: Meulenhoff, 1947.

Wilder, Amos N. *Early Christian Rhetoric.* London: SCM, 1964.
Young, Archibald M. "Some Aspects of St. Augustine's Literary Aesthetics, studied chiefly in *De Doctrina Christiana.*" *Harvard Theological Review*, 62 (1969), pp. 289–299.